KidCoder™ Series

KidCoder™: Windows Programming

Student Textbook

Second Edition

Copyright 2010

Homeschool Programming, Inc.

KidCoder™: Windows Programming

ISBN: **978-0-9830749-0-8**

Terms of Use

This course is copyright protected. Copyright 2010 © Homeschool Programming, Inc. Purchase of this course constitutes your agreement to the Terms of Use. You are not allowed to distribute any part of the course materials by any means to anyone else. You are not allowed to make it available for free (or fee) on any other source of distribution media, including the Internet, by means of posting the file, or a link to the file on newsgroups, forums, blogs or any other location. You may reproduce (print or copy) course materials as needed for your personal use only.

Disclaimer

Homeschool Programming, Inc, and their officers and shareholders, assume no liability for damage to personal computers or loss of data residing on personal computers arising due to the use or misuse of this course material. Always follow instructions provided by the manufacturer of 3rd party programs that may be included or referenced by this course.

Contact Us

You may contact Homeschool Programming, Inc. through the information and links provided on our website: http://www.HomeschoolProgramming.com. We welcome your comments and questions regarding this course or other related programming courses you would like to study!

Other Courses

Homeschool Programming, Inc. currently has two product lines for students: the KidCoder™ series and the TeenCoder™ series. Our KidCoder™ series provides easy, step-by-step programming curriculum for 4th through 8th graders. These courses use Visual Basic to teach introductory programming concepts in a fun, graphical manner. Our TeenCoder™ series provides introductory programming curriculum for high-school students. These courses are college-preparatory material designed for the student who may wish to pursue a career in Computer Science or enhance their transcript with a technical elective.

3rd Party Copyrights

This course uses Microsoft's Visual Basic 2010 Express as the programming platform. Visual Studio, Visual Studio Express, Windows, and all related products are copyright of Microsoft Corporation. Please see http://www.microsoft.com/express/default.aspx for more details.

Instructional Videos

This course may be accompanied by optional Instructional Videos! These Flash-based videos will play directly from a DVD drive on the student's computer. Instructional Videos are supplements to the Student Textbook, covering every chapter and lesson with fun, animated re-enforcement of the main topics.

Instructional Videos are intended for students who enjoy a more audio-visual style of learning. They are not replacements for the Student Textbook which is still required to complete this course! However by watching the Instructional Videos first, students may begin each textbook chapter and lesson already having some grasp of the material to be read. Where applicable, the videos will also show "screencasts" of a real programmer demonstrating some concept or activity within the software development environment.

This Student Textbook and accompanying material are entirely sufficient to complete the course successfully! Instructional Videos are optional for students who would benefit from the alternate presentation of the material. For more information or to purchase the videos separately, please refer to the product descriptions on our website: http://www.HomeschoolProgramming.com.

Table of Contents

Before You Begin

Please read the following topics before you begin the course.

Minimum Hardware and Software Requirements

This is a hands-on programming course. You will be installing Microsoft's Visual Basic 2010 Express software on your computer. Your computer must meet the following minimum requirements in order to run Visual Basic 2010 Express:

Computer Hardware

Your computer must meet the following minimum specifications:

	Minimum
CPU	1.6GHz or faster processor
RAM	1024 MB
Display	1024 x 768 Direct-X compatible video card
Hard Disk Speed	5400 RPM or faster
Hard Disk Size	3GB available space
DVD Drive	DVD-ROM drive

Operating Systems

Your computer operating system must match one of the following:

Windows XP (x86) with Service Pack 3 or above
Windows Vista (x86 and x64) with Service Pack 2 or above
Windows 7 (x86 and x64)
Windows Server 2003 (x86 and x64) with Service Pack 2 or above
Windows Server 2003 R2 (x86 and x64)
Windows Server 2008 (x86 and x64) with Service Pack 2 or above
Windows Server 2008 R2 (x64)

Conventions Used in This Text

This course will use certain styles (fonts, borders, etc) to highlight text of special interest.

```
Source code will be in 11-point Consolas font, in a single box like this.
```

Variable names will be in **12-point Consolas bold** text, similar to the way they will look in your development environment. For example: **myVariable**.

Function and subroutine names, properties, and keywords will be in **bold face** type, so that they are easily readable.

This picture highlights important concepts within a lesson.

Sidebars may contain additional information, tips, or background material.

A chapter review section is included at the end of each chapter.

Every chapter includes a "Your Turn" activity that allows you to practice the ideas you have learned in a real program.

What You Will Learn and Do In This Course

KidCoder[TM]*: Windows Programming* will teach you the basics of writing your own computer programs. This course is written for elementary and middle-school students who have an interest in computer programming.

This course will not teach you how to make a cool webpage or write a 3D game using 10 lines of script. To do those things you are using *someone else's* application to handle most of the work. Here you will learn to write *your own* programs and begin to understand the building blocks for other applications that you may use every day!

Starting with Chapter 2, each chapter will include a walk-through of a program that demonstrates the concepts that you are learning. At the end of each chapter, you will get a chance to add something to each program on your own.

What You Need to Know Before Starting

You are expected to already know the basics of computer use before beginning this course. You need to know how to use the keyboard and mouse to select and run programs, use application menu systems, and work with the Windows operating system. You should understand how to store and load files on your hard disk, and how to use the Windows Explorer to walk through your file system and directory structures. You should also have some experience with using text editors and using web browsers to find helpful information on the Internet.

Software Versions

You will be using the *Microsoft Visual Basic 2010 Express* software to complete this course. This program can be freely downloaded from Microsoft's website. Your course will contain download and install instructions in PDF format. Microsoft may from time to time change their website or download process, or release newer versions of the product. Please refer to http://www.HomeschoolProgramming.com as needed for the latest instructions!

Getting Help & Course Errata

All courses come with a Solution Guide PDF and fully coded solutions for all activities! Simply install the "Solution Files" from your course setup program and you will be able to refer to the solutions as needed from the "Solution Menu". If you are confused about any activity you can see how we solved the problem!

We welcome your feedback regarding any course details that are unclear or that may need correction. You can find a list of course errata for this edition on our website.

Chapter One: Introduction to Computers

Welcome to the *KidCoder*^{TM}*: Windows Programming* course! In this course you will learn how to write your own computer programs using the Visual Basic programming language. The first chapter contains information on computer hardware, software, and the history of programming.

Lesson One: A Little Bit About Computers

We'll start this course at the beginning. To really understand *where* we are going with computers, you need to understand *how* computers were invented in the first place. First let's define the term: *computer*.

Some people think of a computer as any machine that computes. This definition is pretty fuzzy, and may include too many machines that really don't fit the modern idea of the computer. For this reason, we will consider a computer to be an electronic machine that can store, retrieve and process digital information and that can be programmed with instructions.

Based on this definition, the first true computer was something called the ENIAC (**E**lectronic **N**umerical **I**ntegrator **A**nd **C**omputer), created in Pennsylvania in the early 1940s. This computer was the first high-speed, purely electronic, digital computer which could be programmed and re-programmed to handle many different jobs. This machine's main goals were to calculate artillery firing tables for the US Army's Ballistic Research Laboratory, to make atomic energy calculations and to predict weather.

So, what was the ENIAC like? A big desktop computer? A large console? Nope. It was a monster! The ENIAC lived in boxes that were 8.5 feet high and 3 feet wide. There were enough of these boxes to stretch 80 feet long. All told, the computer took up 680 square feet of space and weighed in at just over 30 short tons.

ENIAC's important advantage over earlier machines was its ability to be *re-programmed* by a machine operator. This was done by changing a series of switches and cables on the sides of the device. This ability made this machine truly advanced for its age. However, re-programming the ENIAC was a difficult task. The process started with ideas, which were turned into flowcharts, which were followed by detailed engineering documents and finally the boring and lengthy process of physically re-wiring the machine.

To program the ENIAC, the Army used what it called six "computers". These computers were all women, whose job was to manually change the over 3000 electrical switches on the ENIAC. These women were vital to the programming of the ENIAC and many went on to important roles in the development of present-day software.

So, how did we get from tons of wires and switches to today's personal computer? We can thank two important inventions for our smaller, powerful computers. These two inventions were the *stored program computer* and the *transistor*.

The stored program computer was invented by a man named von Neumann in 1948. This new computer could store programs in computer memory rather than on hard-wired switches. These computers were easier and faster to re-program to do different jobs. Now instead of days, it took just a few hours to completely re-program a computer.

The von Neumann machines were a great advancement in programming, but did nothing to fix the problem of a computer's size and cost. The common computer in the 1940s and 1950s was about the size of a room and could cost millions of dollars - not exactly a cheap home computer!

The second invention to revolutionize the computer industry was the transistor. A transistor is a semiconductor device used to boost or switch electronic signals. Old computers used vacuum tubes to carry signals. Vacuum tubes were large and tended to run very hot. Transistors are more flexible, smaller and more reliable than vacuum tubes and ran much cooler. Also, transistors could be created quickly and cheaply, leading to smaller, more reliable, mass-produced computers.

Eventually, large groups of transistors became the microprocessors which you can find in everything from computers to microwave ovens. Transistors have continued to become smaller and smaller, allowing for more and more circuits, resulting in faster and more powerful microprocessors. These smaller processors lead to smaller computers, like our desktop computers, laptop computers, and even handheld computers!

Today, computers are everywhere. They are in our cell phones, PDAs, MP3 players and remote controls! Any electronic device that can save your information when it is turned off is most likely a computer. How many computers do you think you have in your house?

Lesson Two: Computer Hardware

The term *hardware* refers to all the physical parts of the computer system. In this lesson we will discuss the major pieces of hardware in your desktop computer.

Case

The computer case is the external shell that holds all other computer components. The case usually contains one or more cooling fans to keep the internal components from getting too hot.

Motherboard

The most important part of a computer is the *motherboard*. The motherboard acts like the body of the computer – it is the central point where all the other components connect together. The motherboard contains the Central Processing Unit (CPU), the RAM (memory) and all the connectors for other devices like the mouse, keyboard, etc.

Video Card

In order to show programs and data on a computer screen, you must have a video card. This device makes all of the images you see on the monitor. Sometimes, a video card is built into the motherboard. In other cases, the video card is a separate card which is plugged into the motherboard. Usually the add-on cards are much better quality than the built-in devices.

Sound Card

The computer's sound card has become a very important feature in the last 10-15 years. It sends sound effects and music to the computer's speakers. A sound card is also used to capture sound with a microphone or a Line-In connection. Like the video card, a sound card can be built into the motherboard or plugged in as a separate card. Also like the video card, an add-on sound card usually has better quality and more features.

Hard Disk

The main storage on a computer is called the hard disk. Hard disks save programs and data inside the PC, remembering everything even when the power is turned off. Programs and data are arranged into folders (directories) and files on the disk. Hard disks store information magnetically on a series of circular platters that spin at high speed.

Removable Media

In order to bring new programs or data to a computer, many types of removable media can be inserted into the computer. Once, the only device of this type was the floppy disk, but those times are far behind us! Now a computer can have many devices attached to its motherboard: CD-ROMs, DVD-ROMs, Zip drives, tape drives and even the small, ultra-portable USB flash drives.

Peripherals

The last kind of hardware you can attach to a computer is called a peripheral. Peripherals are the input and output devices that are connected externally to the computer. Some common input devices are the keyboard, mouse, webcam, scanner, microphone, or game controller. Some common output devices are the printer, monitor, or speakers.

Lesson Three: Computer Software

The software on a computer is the collection of programs that make the computer work. There are three types of software programs: Operating Systems, Device Drivers, and Applications.

Operating Systems

The operating system is the underlying software that makes it possible to run other programs on the computer. It ties together all of the hardware components and gives the user a way to control the computer. The three main operating systems on the market today are: UNIX, Mac OS and Microsoft Windows.

UNIX was one of the first operating systems for the modern desktop computer. Originally created in the 1960s, UNIX was the first operating system to allow more than one user to run different programs at the same time. This made it very fast and powerful. However, UNIX is difficult to learn and use. Therefore, although it is still popular today in certain industries (especially the free Linux version), UNIX is not widely used by the general public.

The Mac operating systems run the Apple line of computers. The most current Mac OS is called OS X or OS Ten. This operating system is based on Unix BSD, which is a common flavor of UNIX. The Mac operating systems have always prided themselves on ease of use and solid reliability. In recent years, Mac OS has also experienced fewer security issues than Microsoft Windows. However, there is not as much software available for Mac OS in comparison to the other operating systems.

The Microsoft Windows operating system is perhaps the most common operating system used today. This is most likely the operating system that you have on your own computer and is the operating system that we will be using to create and run our programs in this class!

Device Drivers

Device drivers are small pieces of software that work at a low level within the operating system. The purpose of a device driver is to make a piece of hardware such as mouse or printer work with the operating system. Just because you plug in some fancy new printer doesn't mean your computer can use it right away! You may first have to install a device driver that knows how to talk with the printer. Once you install the device driver, then you can use the printer from one of your applications!

Applications

Applications are any kind of software that runs on top of the operating system. There are many kinds of applications covering nearly every imaginable topic. Applications are the software that you typically work with as a computer user. Common applications include business software like spreadsheets and word processors, educational software like writing and math programs, and even fun software like screensavers and computer games.

The Microsoft Visual Basic 2010 Express software, which we will use to create programs in this class, is a type of application software. This software is usually called an IDE (Integrated Development Environment), which helps programmers by allowing them to easily design, write and debug programs in one application.

Lesson Four: Programming Languages

What language does your computer speak? It doesn't speak English, or Spanish or French. Your computer only speaks one native language: Machine Language. This language is a *binary* language, as it only uses two symbols: the numbers 0 and 1.

So, can you program your computer in machine language? Absolutely! But it would take a long time and a lot of work to write a program using 1s and 0s. Instead, we use *higher level* programming languages. These languages allow us to write a program in *human-readable* form called *source code*. When the source code is completed a *compiler* program takes care of changing the human-readable source into machine language.

In this course, we will be using Visual Basic, a modern, high-level language. This language allows you to use English-like words and phrases to tell a computer what to do. Visual Basic is very easy to learn and is widely used throughout the programming industry.

Elements of a Programming Language

A programming language is fully defined by its *specification*. A language specification typically contains a number of key elements: format (syntax), data types, and a common library.

The *format* or *syntax* of a programming language describes the possible combinations of letters or symbols that are used to form statements and expressions in a program. The format of most programming languages uses expressions similar to a natural spoken language. With well-written code, these larger expressions should be easily readable and understood by humans.

Data types are the programming language's ways to describe kinds of data. In programming, there may be numeric data, text data, character data, and so on. Each data type is stored and processed differently. We will talk more about data types in a future chapter.

Libraries are blocks of code that do common tasks. These blocks of code are commonly referred to as *functions*. For example, in Visual Basic, there is a common library function to show a message pop-up window. Instead of writing the code to show the window every time you need it, you just use the common function. Re-using existing functions makes programs easier to write and smaller in size.

Functions make programmer's jobs much easier by creating groups of code that perform special tasks. These functions usually handle common tasks like printing data to the screen or writing data to a file. A programmer can then use these functions instead of having to write the code themselves.

History of Programming Languages

Although computers have been around since the early 1900s, programming languages have only existed since the 1940s. It was during the time that our country was busy fighting World War II that some of the early research and development in programming languages occurred.

As computers became more powerful, so did the programming languages that supported them. In the 1940s, programmers began to switch from the 1s and 0s of machine language to languages like Assembler, which used simple words and phrases. In the 1950s and 1960s, languages continued to improve for use with mainframe computers. High-level languages like COBOL allowed programmers more flexibility and easier programming with more English-like syntax. The BASIC language (an early form of Visual Basic) was created during these years.

In the 1970s and 1980s, we began to see a switch to modern programming languages like "C", which uses functions to group common code together and provides powerful pre-built libraries. Early home computers were able to run many programs written in high-level languages like C.

In the 1990s, one invention reshaped our world: the Internet. The Internet came with a whole set of problems for programmers and programming languages. An Internet browser was capable of running programs downloaded from web servers, but not the kinds of programs that had existed before this time.

Now there were programs where the original code (the HTML web page) existed on a server in a remote location and an application (the web browser) was on the user's computer. *Scripted* languages such as JavaScript and display languages such as HTML were developed to control the behavior of the web browser.

Programming languages continue to evolve today. One current area of concern is security. As the Internet becomes more available and our computers are connected to it for longer time periods, we have a greater need for security. Connection to the outside world is a great feature, but the downside is that, in some ways, the outside world has access to our computers as well. Programming languages today are making changes to add more security features to protect both users and programmers.

Chapter Review

- A *computer* is an electronic machine that can store, retrieve and process digital information and that can be programmed with instructions.

- The ENIAC was the first true computer

- Modern computers were made possible with the help of two important inventions: the *stored-program* computer and the *transistor*.

- The term *hardware* refers to the physical parts of a computer. *Software* refers to the collection of programs that makes the computer work.

- The three main groups of software are operating systems, device drivers, and applications.

- Computers speak machine language, which is difficult to program in native 1's and 0's.

- High-level programming languages use human-readable syntax to program a computer.

- BASIC, an early form of Visual Basic, was created in the 1960s.

- We will be using the Windows operating system and Microsoft Visual Basic 2010 Express software to write the computer programs in this course.

Your Turn: Install Visual Basic 2010 Express

In this activity you will be installing the course files, the Microsoft Visual Basic 2010 Express software and the MSDN Help Library on your computer.

Course files	The files that come with this course include material for the student (chapter sample programs, activity starters, instructional documents) and for the teacher (activity solutions, tests, answer keys, etc).
Visual Basic 2010 Express	This software is a free student version of the professional Visual Studio product. Visual Studio is a popular example of an IDE, or Integrated Development Environment. This is a very important piece of software for any programmer! An IDE is the central place where you will create, compile, run, and debug your program.
MSDN Help Library	The MSDN Help Library is an integrated reference system that allows programmers to quickly pull up help on functions and programming concepts from within the IDE.

Installing the Course Files

The files for this course are installed by a single setup executable that came with your course purchase. The setup file is called "KidCoder_WindowsProgramming.exe" (or similar name). Ensure that you are running a Windows account with administrative privileges on your machine when you launch the setup executable.

The setup executable will offer you the choice of installing the Student Files and/or Solution Files. You may install these components on the same computer (if the student should have free access to the solutions) or on different computers (so the teacher can maintain control over the solutions).

Go ahead and perform this setup process now. We recommend installing to the default "C:\KidCoder\Windows Programming" directory as we will refer to that directory structure throughout the textbook. You may choose an alternate location if desired. The setup program will automatically create a "My Projects" directory under the target installation – this is where all of the student projects will go!

Once installation is complete you will have a new "KidCoder" group on your Windows Start Menu. Underneath "KidCoder" is a "Windows Programming" folder. Within that folder are one or two menus for the Student and Solution files (depending on your choices during setup). The look and feel of the Windows Start Menu changes between versions of Windows, but your final menu system should look something like this (assuming both Student and Solution files installed):

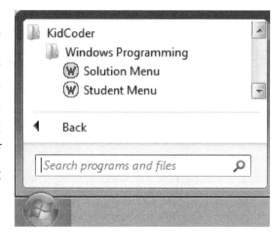

You can run these menus for convenient, graphical access to all of the instructional documents (PDFs), activity solutions, and other material distributed with the course. You may also simply run Windows Explorer and navigate to your target install directory (C:\KidCoder\Windows Programming) and launch these files on your own! Use of the Menu systems is optional. Here is an example screen shot from Windows Explorer that shows the directory structure and files in your target directory (details may vary).

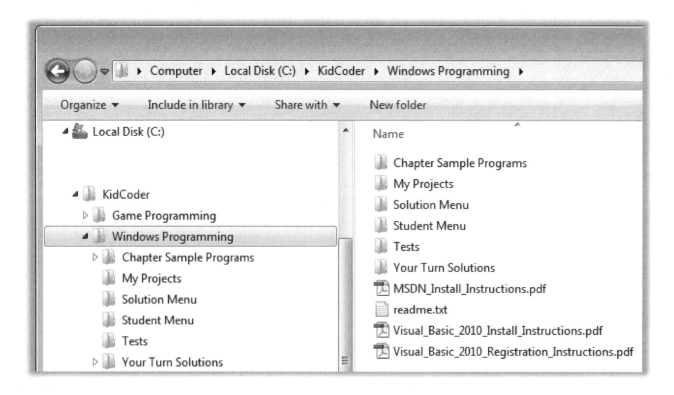

A ".PDF" file is a common document format that requires the free Adobe Acrobat program to read. Your computer should already have the Acrobat reader installed. If you cannot view the PDF documents, you will need to install Acrobat reader first from http://get.adobe.com/reader/.

Installing Visual Basic 2010 Express

Your next major activity is to install the Visual Basic 2010 Express software on your computer. You will need to be connected to the Internet during the installation of Visual Basic 2010 Express. Always ask your teacher before doing any activity online! Now, let's get started!

Your course includes a document named "Visual_Basic_2010_Install_Instructions.pdf" which contains complete, step-by-step instructions on downloading and installing the software.

Please open the "Visual Basic Install Instructions.pdf" document now, either through the Student Menu or by launching the PDF directly from Windows Explorer, and follow the instructions to install the IDE on your computer. Within 30 days of installation you also need to register with Microsoft (a free process), so we recommend you do that now as well. Please read and complete the instructions in the "Visual_Basic_2010_Registration_Instructions.pdf" document to register your software with Microsoft.

Getting Help!

Very often you will want to get help on an error, or function description, or some other part of Visual Studio or the Visual Basic programming language. The MSDN (Microsoft Developer Network) Library, a great help tool, can be installed on top of Visual Studio. Then, to get help on any topic, just position the mouse in the IDE on the item in question (like a compiler error number or function name) and hit the F1 key. If help files are not installed locally MSDN will go online to get help for you.

Please find the "MSDN_Install_Instructions.pdf" document in your course materials and follow those instructions now to install the MSDN help library.

You can also use many online resources to help find solutions to error messages or understand the meaning of certain Visual Basic topics. Any of the major search engines will lead you to dozens of topics on programming and Visual Studio. Some well-established sites such as Wikipedia (http://www.wikipedia.com) also offer good articles on many programming topics.

The Working Directory for Projects

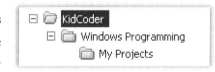

After installing the course files, a "My Projects" directory was automatically created for you. This directory will be the location where you will save all of your projects for this course. The default directory structure is "C:\KidCoder\Windows Programming\My Projects". Each project you create should be placed in a new sub-folder within your working directory. You may select a different working directory or even create additional working directories on your own; just remember your directory location when you want to save and load your projects. Multiple students may use the same computer for this course by creating different working directories! Use the Windows Explorer program to create new directories.

Chapter Two: Get Your Feet Wet

It's time to start learning the Visual Basic programming language! This chapter will describe the language, the development environment, and walk you step-by-step through the creation of your first program.

Lesson One: Introducing Visual Basic

The Visual Basic programming language grew out of an older language called BASIC. BASIC, which stands for **B**eginner's **A**ll-purpose **S**ymbolic **I**nstruction **C**ode, was created in 1964. This language was very popular from the late 60s to the late 80s mainly because it was so easy to use. This language finally made it possible for the average person to program a computer!

The BASIC language was created in 1964 at Dartmouth College in New Hampshire. At that time, all programming on campus was done by the Science and Math students, who were the only ones to understand the complex computer languages. BASIC was created to allow non-science students to easily write their own computer programs.

In the 1980s, Apple Computer came out with a new graphical computer interface called "Lisa". Microsoft quickly came out with their own version of a graphical system called Windows. These graphical operating systems were called GUIs, and they revolutionized the computer industry.

What is GUI? GUI stands for "**G**raphical **U**ser **I**nterface". This means that instead of using computers by typing text at a command-line, now users could see graphical images of files and data. This type of operating system allows a user to manage a computer through point-and-click graphics, icons and other visual aids. Most of the programs that you use today are GUI programs.

With the introduction of Microsoft Windows, there came a need for more graphical applications. There were many complicated languages that could create Windows applications, but few that could do it quickly or easily. Microsoft created the Visual Basic language, similar to BASIC, to fill this gap. Visual Basic allowed programmers to quickly put together simple Windows applications. In minutes, a programmer can have a Windows program up and running!

Through the last 20 years, Visual Basic has continued to evolve. More and more functionality and abilities have been added, like database programming and web-based programming. The Visual Basic language is widely used today in both schools and businesses. The most current version of Visual Basic is called Visual Basic.Net (pronounced "dot-net"). This is the version that comes with the Visual Basic 2010 Express software and is the version that we will be using for this course.

Why are we Using Visual Basic?

Why Visual Basic? Well, to be honest, it's just plain fun! The Visual Basic programming language is an easy-to-learn language that allows you to create Windows applications very quickly and easily. In addition, this is a serious programming language that is widely-used today in colleges and businesses. A big attraction of the Visual Basic language is its ability to do RAD programming. RAD stands for **R**apid-**A**pplication **D**evelopment. Typically, in the business world, this means Visual Basic is used to create *prototypes*. Prototypes are what programmers use to test a program idea by creating a quick test application. Many businesses use the Visual Basic language to create these test applications.

Another reason to love the Visual Basic language is that, while famous for its simple Windows programs, it can also be used to create more complex programs. This course will teach you much of the fundamentals of the Visual Basic language. In addition, we will give you pointers for how to make your programs more complex – how to build your simple applications into more full-featured applications.

Lesson Two: Visual Basic Development Environment

The main software package that we will be using in this course is called *Visual Basic 2010 Express*. This program is also called an IDE (**I**ntegrated **D**evelopment **E**nvironment). In the early days of programming, a programmer would write their code in one application, build the program in another application, and test it in yet another application. Today, programmers have Integrated Development Environments. The IDE is a single place where you can create your screens, type in your code, and run and debug your program. Everything you need as a programmer can be found in your IDE.

Let's take a look at your Visual Basic IDE, which you installed at the end of the last chapter. To start the application, click on your Windows Start button. Then find the icon for "Microsoft Visual Basic 2010 Express". This is the Visual Basic IDE, so go ahead and run it! Your Windows Start menu may look different depending on the version of Windows you are running.

Once the program loads, you should see the following screen:

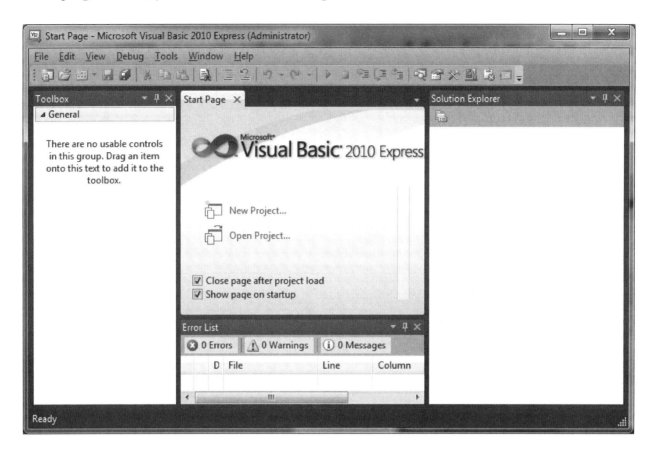

This is the default screen for the IDE. Since we have not yet created any programs, we begin on the "Start Page". From here we can create a new project or open an existing project.

The first thing we will do is create a new *project*. Projects are a way to group together all the screens and files necessary for an application. Each project will make one program (executable, or .EXE file). You will be working on different projects for each of your chapter activities.

To create a project, you can click on the "New Project" line on the Start page, or just click on the "File" menu option and then click on "New Project". You should see the following screen:

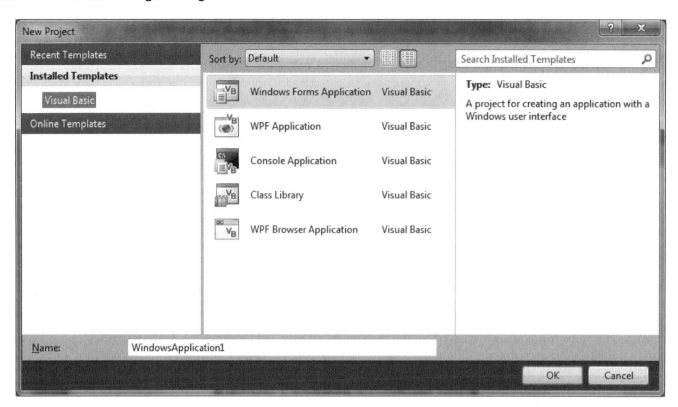

You can create different types of programs with Visual Basic. For this course, we will be using the "Windows Forms Application". This template should be highlighted by default in the middle section. If it is not, just highlight it now by clicking on the top line.

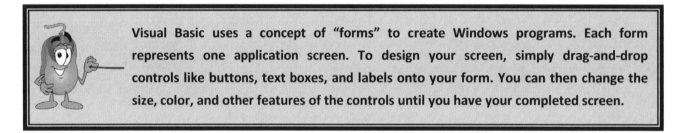

Visual Basic uses a concept of "forms" to create Windows programs. Each form represents one application screen. To design your screen, simply drag-and-drop controls like buttons, text boxes, and labels onto your form. You can then change the size, color, and other features of the controls until you have your completed screen.

The white edit field at the bottom of the screen contains the name of your project. You don't want keep the default name "WindowsApplication1"; every project should be given a separate, meaningful name. For this lesson, just create a project called "Chapter 2" by typing that name into the text box.

Now click the OK button to create your first project. This will bring up the main IDE window. We will go through the items on this screen one at a time.

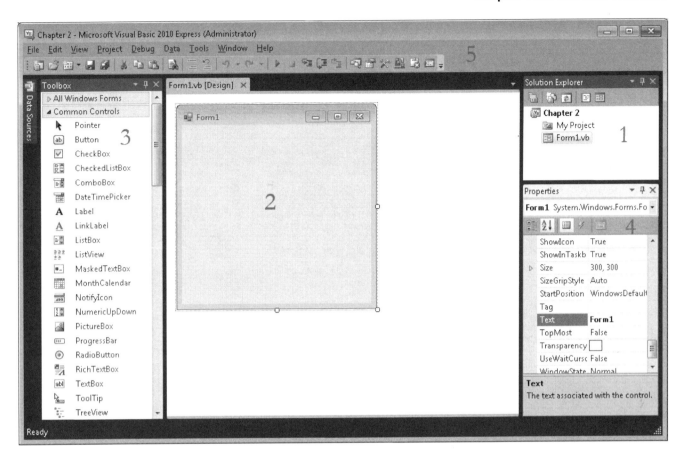

The main IDE window is separated into different frames, just like the panes in a house window. In the picture above we have labeled each pane with the numbers 1 – 5 for easy reference, though those numbers do not show up in the actual application.

You may notice some frames are hidden to start. For instance, if your Toolbox is collapsed onto a small tab, simply click the Toolbox tab so it expands, then click the icon that looks like a thumb-tack (Auto-Hide) to keep the frame visible.

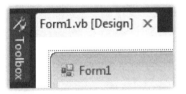
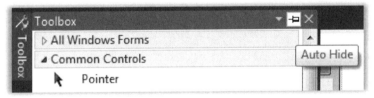

The first frame (#1) that we will look at is the Solution Explorer. If you don't have this frame, look for the icon that looks like this on the toolbar: . This is the Solution Explorer button and will show or hide this frame in the IDE window. The Solution Explorer frame is where you can view and access all the forms or files for your project. In your current Solution Explorer you should see the name of our project, "Chapter 2", and two lines: "My Project" and "Form1.vb". The My Project line represents the settings for this project, which are stored in a file with the ".vbproj" extension. The "Form1.vb" file is your main source code file that represents the form (screen) for the project.

The second frame (#2) is the Form Design frame. This is the "canvas" that you will use to create your screen. Here, you can add controls to your form screen and change how those controls look and behave. If you don't see this frame, you can click on the ⊞ icon in the Solution Explorer. You can also right-click on your "Form1.vb" line and select "View Designer". When you load one of your projects, and you don't see the Form Design frame by default, don't panic! Just follow either of those two methods to show the frame.

When we start to write code for our form, you can click on the ▤ icon in the Solution Explorer to show the code for the form. You can also select the "Form1.vb" line, right-click, and select "View Code".

Go ahead and click on these two icons now to see how you switch back and forth between the Form Design screen and the code window!

The next frame (#3) holds the Controls Toolbox, which is useful when you are showing the Form Design screen in the middle. The Toolbox contains a big list of items that you can put onto your form screen. If you don't see this frame, click on the ⚒ button. This will either show or hide the Toolbox. The Controls Toolbox contains all the controls or elements that you might need to build your Form. These controls are added by simply dragging and dropping the control from the toolbox to the form with your mouse.

Try this now: left-click on the "Button" line in the Toolbox and drag it onto your form.

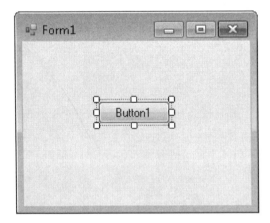

The next frame (#4) is the Properties Sheet frame. If you don't see this frame, click on the ▣ icon, or hit the F4 key or right-click on your button and select "Properties". The Properties Sheet is used to set all of the options for the individual controls or the overall form. For example, if you wanted to change the color, text, or name of a control, you would do it on the Properties Sheet.

Try this now: click on your button and look at the properties available for this control. Find the "Text" property and type "Click" where the property says "Button1". Notice how the text on your button changes!

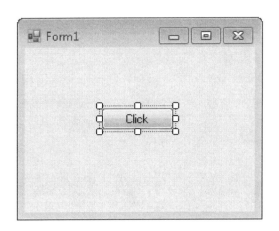
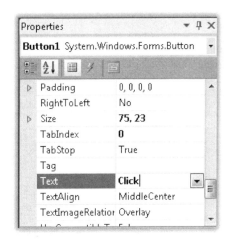

The last section (#5) of the IDE contains the menu bar and toolbar. You are probably familiar with these types of menus and toolbars, since many Windows applications have them. These buttons and menu options are used to control every part of the IDE program. You can open and save new projects and forms, run programs, show or hide frames, close the IDE, and perform other jobs.

Lesson Three: Your First Program

In this lesson, we will be creating your first Visual Basic program! To create this program, we will again be using the Visual Basic IDE. Go ahead and open up this program now.

Once the IDE is open, click on "File" and "New Project". You should see the New Project screen below:

Make sure the Windows Form Application icon is highlighted and name your new project "Hello World". Click on the OK button to finish creating the new project.

You should now see the main IDE window, which should look like the image shown on the next page.

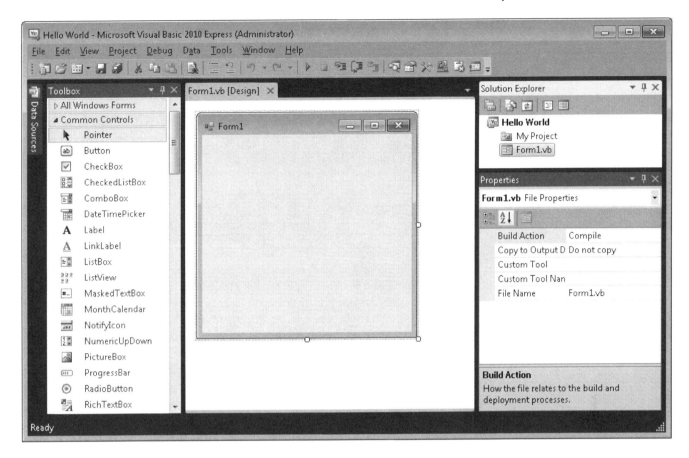

The first thing we will do is change the name of the form. This won't have any visible effect on your form, but each form in your application should have a unique, meaningful name.

Click anywhere on the form to highlight it and then look at the Property Sheet in the lower right corner. In the list of properties, find the property called **(Name)** (this should be near the top of the list). You will notice that in the spot next to **(Name)**, you see the current name "Form1" in bold type. Click on "Form1", and you will see a cursor appear on that line. Go ahead and delete the word "Form1" and put in "MyFirstForm". Congratulations! You have changed your first form property. The **(Name)** property is important when you have more than one form in your program. For now, it's just good practice to give it a meaningful name.

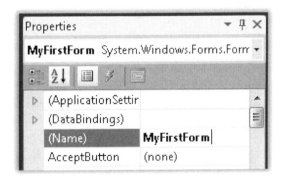

If you look at your form in the main window, you will see that it has a caption (or title) of "Form1". The next thing we are going to do is make that caption a little more interesting!

To change the caption, we need to find the form property called **Text**. Look through the list of properties until you find this item (the list is alphabetical, it will be near the bottom). In the spot next to **Text**, you see the current caption "Form1" in bold type. Click on "Form1", and you will see a cursor appear on that line. Go ahead and delete the word "Form1" and put in "Hello, World". Once you are finished, click back on the form and you will see the caption change!

Now we are going to add a control to your form. For this program, we will add a *label* control. A label is just a simple control that allows you to add some text or words to the screen. To add this control, first find the **Label** in the Controls Toolbox.

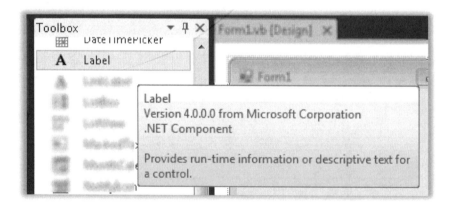

Once you find the **Label**, just left-click and drag it over to your form. Release the mouse click and the label will stick to the form in that spot. Now your form should look like this:

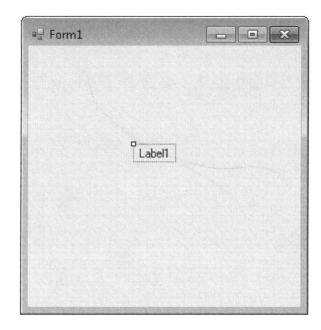

Now let's make the label more interesting! Click on the label on your form to highlight it, and look at the property sheet. You should be looking at the properties for **Label1**. We are going to change the text for this label just like we changed the caption text. Find the property called **Text** that has the value **Label1**. Click on the word **Label1** and change the text to "Hello, World!" Now click on the form again and *voila!* The label now says "Hello, World!"

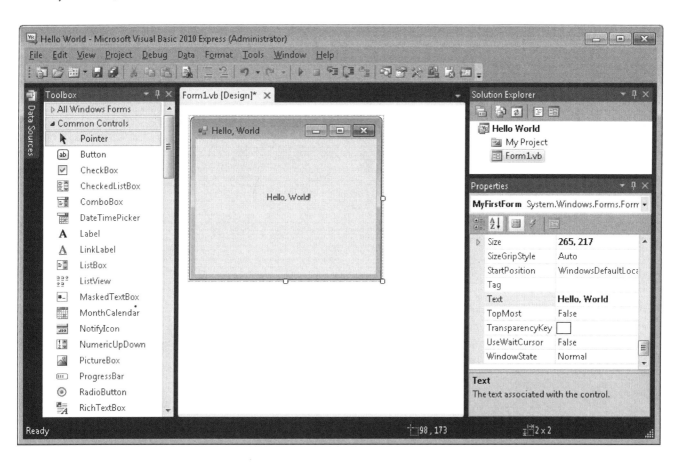

Now, let's run your program! To do this, just find the button on the main toolbar that looks like the play button on a DVD player: ▶ . Click on this button and you should see your program run!

To exit your program, click on the "X" in the upper right corner of the screen, just like in any other Windows program. Congratulations! You have just created your first program in Visual Basic!

Saving Your Project

You should always save your project before you exit the Visual Basic IDE. To do this, click on "File" and "Save All". The IDE will pop-up this window:

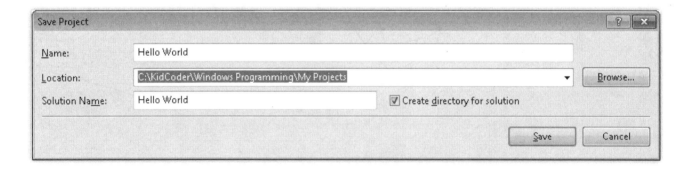

Change the "Location" field to show the working directory you selected for your projects (such as "C:\KidCoder\Windows Programming\My Projects") when installing the course. Then make sure the Solution Name is "Hello World" and then click the "Save" button.

Now when you want to go back to this project, just click on "File" and "Open Project". This will bring up the following window:

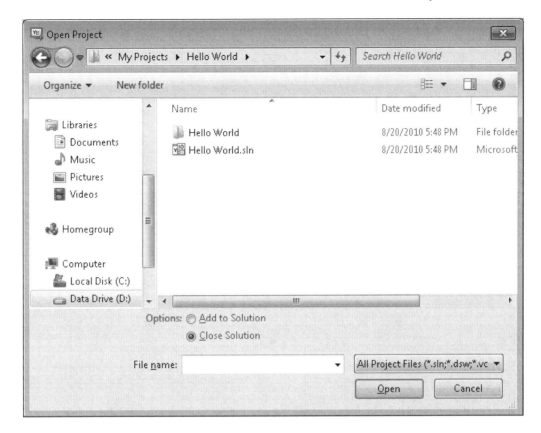

From here, you can find the directory where you saved your project. If you followed the suggested directory structure during installation, you should find your files in: "C:\KidCoder\Windows Programming\My Projects\Hello World". In this case, your project is named "Hello World.sln". If you choose this file and click the "Open" button, your project will open into the IDE program. A .sln file is called a "solution" file and is the main container for all of your project files.

Help! My Work Has Disappeared!

One common mystery for new programmers is the "Case of the Missing Work". It starts when you are working on your project and decide to save your work and close the Visual Basic software. You come back later and open your project in the IDE, only to find that the code window and/or the Form Design window are missing!

The work that you have completed is not gone! It's simply hidden. This is one of the easiest problems to solve. If you are missing your Form design screen, you can click on the ⊞ icon in the Solution Explorer, or press the Shift-F7 keys at the same time or right-click on your "Form1.vb" file and select "View Design". If you are missing your code window, you can click on the ▤ icon in the Solution Explorer or press the F7 key or right-click on "Form1.vb" and select "View Source" to show the code for the form. If you do not see the Solution Explorer on the screen, click on "View" on the top menu and then choose "Other Windows" and then "Solution Explorer".

For some reason, Microsoft may sometimes change the default viewing settings in the Visual Basic software after you register the program, causing the code and Form windows to be "hidden" by default. We recommend that you register the software right after installation!

Understanding Your Project Files

Let's take a closer look at the files and directories inside the "My Projects\Hello World" directory! You can review the project files and subdirectories by using Windows Explorer.

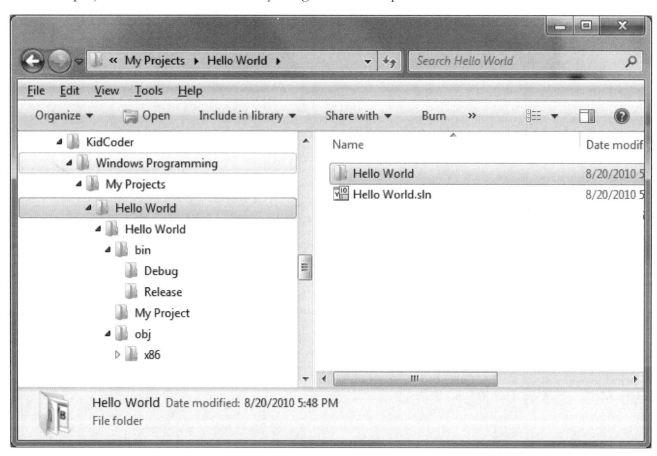

The first thing that you may notice is that there are two folders named "Hello World". The first (highest) "Hello World" folder holds all of the files and information for the "Hello World" program. There is only one file in this folder: "Hello World.sln". This is the overall solution for our program. This solution can hold one or more individual projects. (Although in this course, we will only ever have one project in a solution.)

The second "Hello World" folder contains all of the files for the main project in our program (which is also called "Hello World"). There are three more sub-folders under this "Hello World" folder: "bin", "My Project" and "obj".

The "bin" folder is created the first time you build your program. This is where the Visual Basic software will place the executable (EXE) or fully-compiled version of your program. For this project, the executable file will be called "Hello World.exe". The "Debug" folder will contain the executable version that is run when you launch the program from the IDE. If you simply build the program in the IDE (without running it) then the executable is placed in the "Release" folder.

The "obj" folder is also created the first time you build your program. This folder contains some temporary files that are output when Visual Basic builds your program. You will not need to understand or use these files directly. These files are all maintained and handled by the Visual Basic software.

The "My Project" folder is automatically created as you are writing your program. The files in this folder contain information about how your project looks in the Visual Basic software. You will not need to understand or use these files directly. These files are all maintained and handled by the Visual Basic software.

The second "Hello World" folder also contains many files, including these important ones:

Form1.designer.vb	This file contains your form screen definition and is very important!
Form1.resx	This file contains information about outside resources you have added to the project such as graphics, sounds, or other languages.
Form1.vb	This file contains your form's source code and is what you will spend most of your time writing!
Hello World.vbproj	This file contains your project settings.

If you are ever concerned about saving your source code, or sending it to someone else for review, these are the most important files to copy!

Making a Copy of Your Project

You may want to make a copy of your project, especially if you just completed something important and want to make a backup copy. The easiest way to do this is using Windows Explorer, and not the Visual Basic IDE!

To make a backup copy of your project, simply run Windows Explorer and find your project directory (e.g. "My Projects\Hello World"). Then drag or copy that entire folder to a different folder name such as "My Projects\Hello World Backup". That's it! You now have two copies of your project...one in "Hello World" and one in "Hello World Backup". You can change and run each of these projects without messing up the code you have in the other project.

 **Chapter Review**

- The BASIC language was created in the mid-1960s. Visual Basic was adapted from BASIC.

- GUI stands for "Graphical User Interface" and refers to the screens, windows, buttons, and other visual objects that we see on our computer screen.

- An IDE, or "Integrated Development Environment", is a piece of software that allows a programmer to create, design, run and test a program in a single place.

- The Visual Basic IDE is broken into 5 main frames, or parts: the Solution Explorer, the Forms window, the Control Toolbox, the Properties Sheet and the Menu and Toolbar.

- A "solution file" contains information about an entire Visual Basic project.

- Creating a program in Visual Basic is easy, quick and fun!

- You can always pull up your Form Design screen, or form source code, by using the icons available to you in the Solution Explorer.

Your Turn: Hello, Again

In this activity, you will open the Hello World project and get some practice adding controls and changing the properties of forms and controls.

Open up the "Hello World" project from this chapter. To do this, run the Visual Basic IDE and click on "File" and "Open Project" from the menu. Your project should have been saved in "C:\KidCoder\Windows Programming\My Projects\Hello World" and the filename should be "Hello World.sln". Select this file to open the project. If you do not see your project's screen and code in the IDE, use one of the methods described in the chapter to show the screen and code panes.

Here is a list of things that you should try to do with your form:

- Change the **BackColor** property of the form to a different color.

- Change the text of the "Hello World" label.

- Add a button to the form and change the **Text** of the button.

- Add a checkbox to the form and change the **Text** for the checkbox

Run your program and test your changes! Your new form might look something like this:

Chapter Three: Exploring Visual Basic Programs

In the last chapter, we created your first program. Now let's look at some of the key elements of all Visual Basic applications.

Lesson One: Common Graphical Elements

Visual Basic allows programmers to easily define Graphical User Interfaces (GUIs). This lesson will describe some common graphical controls and how they fit into windows on the screen.

Forms

A central feature of any Windows application is the graphical window itself. In many other languages, it takes a great deal of code to create a window or screen in a program. If a program has more than one window, the code is more complex. Adding controls like buttons, text boxes, or checkboxes to this window requires you to write even more code.

The Visual Basic language makes this process much easier! Visual Basic applications are built around an object called a "Form". Forms are windows that are already created for you. You simply add your controls by dragging-and-dropping them from the Toolbox onto the form. Designing your own window is as easy as creating a picture in a drawing program.

The form is the most important graphical element in Visual Basic.. All of the programs that we will write in this course will be based on forms. Every time you create a new project, Visual Basic will supply you with a simple form, which we will change to fit your program's needs.

Controls

Controls are graphical widgets that you can place on the form for a person to use. Visual Basic contains over 40 controls in the Controls Toolbox. From the Toolbox you can easily add buttons, toolbars, menus, text boxes, printing controls, pictures, checkboxes, etc.

Controls are added to a form by simply dragging and dropping the control from the Control Toolbox to the form. All controls have properties, which are settings that determine how the control will look and behave. Once you place a control on the form, you can change the color, shape, and text of your control by changing its properties. The Property Sheet is typically located at the bottom right of the IDE window. If it is not on the screen, you can hit the F4 key to show this sheet at any time. The Property Sheet is a list of all the possible changes you can make to a control. You can quickly modify your control by just clicking on the property and entering a new value; no need to write any code!

Let's look at some of the more popular form controls:

A very common control is the Button. Buttons exist in just about every Windows program. They let the user save work, accept changes, open files, and run other commands. Most actions that can be taken in a program are activated when the user clicks on a button.

Another popular control is the Textbox. Textboxes allow a user to enter text into a program. You can use a textbox to gather text-based information like names and addresses, or user IDs and passwords.

Just as the textbox is useful for allowing a user to enter text, a label control is useful when the program needs to display text for the user. Labels are most often used to describe other controls so that the user knows how to use the form. For example, if you have a textbox on the screen, you might use a label control to tell the user to enter their name.

Another type of control is the option control. Option controls enable a user to make a choice between several items. There are two main types of these controls: Radio buttons and Checkboxes.

Radio buttons offer user a choice between *one* of several options. Each radio label is next to a white circle. When the user selects a label by left-clicking the mouse on the circle, a dot will appear in the circle. Only one option can be selected in a group of radio buttons.

A checkbox also offers the user a choice of options, but this time they can select zero, one or more of these options. Each checkbox label is next to a white box. When the user selects a label by left-clicking the mouse cursor on the box, a check will appear in the box.

There are many other types of controls that you can add to your form – list boxes, drop-down selection boxes, tree controls, and more -- too many to cover in one lesson!

Lesson Two: Visual Basic Syntax

Each computer programming language has rules about how a program can be written. These rules are called the format or *syntax* of the language. If you do not follow the syntax rules of the programming language, your program will not run!

Common Visual Basic Syntax

The Visual Basic syntax is fairly simple compared to other programming languages. For starters, it does not care if you use capital or lower-case letters. Most other languages will see a difference between the words "Function" and "function". Visual Basic, however, will treat these two words as the same thing.

Visual Basic code is written as a series of statements, or lines of code. How does Visual Basic know that you have reached the end of a statement? Once you hit the "Enter" key to move to the next line in your program, Visual Basic knows that you are done with that statement. Here is an example statement:

```
myNumber = 1 + 2
```

In almost every other language a special character such as a semi-colon (;) is used to end a statement. But Visual Basic is happy to end the statement when you press Enter.

What if you have a really long statement? There are two ways to handle this: First, you can put the entire statement on one line. The Visual Basic IDE will allow you to write as long a line as you need. Of course, when viewing this line in the IDE, you will have to scroll the window to see the full code.

Another way of writing a long line of code is to break up the statement into two or more lines. You can't just press "Enter" to break up a line like this, however:

```
myNumber =
1 + 2
```

Visual Basic will view this as two lines of code: "**myNumber=**" and "**1 + 2**"...neither of which makes any sense by itself. As soon as you try to build a program with these lines you will get an error. To fix this you can add an underscore (_) character at the end of a line. The underscore character tells Visual Basic that this statement is continued on the next line. You can break up a single statement into as many lines as you need, as long as you put the underscore character at the end of the line. For example:

```
myNumber _
= _
1 + 2
```

These three lines are understood by Visual Basic as "**myNumber = 1 + 2**".

Another key part of Visual Basic syntax is the comment line. Comments are lines of text that programmers use to tell anyone reading their program what the program is doing. These are plain text lines and contain no program code at all. Visual Basic uses the (') character (a single apostrophe) to identify a comment line. There are no syntax rules for the text you type within a comment. Let's look at some comments and contrast them to program statements:

```
'This is a comment line
'This is another comment. The next line is a program statement.
myNumber = 1 + 2
```

Comments are often used in programs to explain in simple terms what the nearby statements are doing:

```
'Here we calculate the area of a rectangle
myArea = length * width
```

Visual Basic will ignore any line that starts with the apostrophe (') character and there are no limits to the number of comments you can make. It is good practice to add clear comments to your program!

Lesson Three: Responding to Button Clicks

In this lesson we are going to add to your Hello World application by adding a button to the form and then creating code that will run when the user clicks the button.

Go ahead and open up the Visual Basic IDE. Once it has opened, create a new project called "Hello World2". When your new project is open, first change the form's caption to "Hello, World". Highlight the form by clicking on it and then find the **Text** property in the Property Sheet frame. Change the text from "Form1" to "Hello, World". We will also change the **(Name)** of our form to "MyForm". Highlight the form by clicking on it and then find the **(Name)** property in the Property Sheet frame. Change the text from "Form1" to "MyForm".

Next, look at the Controls Toolbar and find the **Button** control. Create a button on your form by dragging and dropping it onto your form. Your form should now look something like this:

The button controls have some of the same properties as the form control. For starters, we are going to change the **Text** property of your button. To do this, first select the button and then look for the **Text** property in the button's Property Sheet. Change "Button1" to "Click Here". We will also change the **(Name)** of our button. Highlight the button and then look for the **(Name)** property in the Property Sheet frame. Change the **(Name)** from "Button1" to "MyButton".

Now your form should look like this:

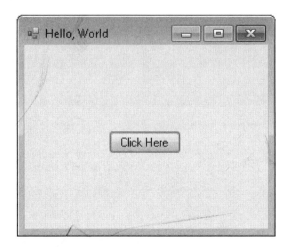

Now that we have your button created and looking good, it's time to make it do something!

When creating forms and using controls in Visual Basic, your program will be *event-driven*. Your program will receive events when actions are taken by the user. This means a specific part of your code called a *function* will be run when an event happens. A function is a collection of one or more statements that do something useful.

Continuing with the example, we want our button to respond to a *button-click* event. To do this, just double-click on the button on your form. A new window should appear in place of your form, and you should see code created for you like this:

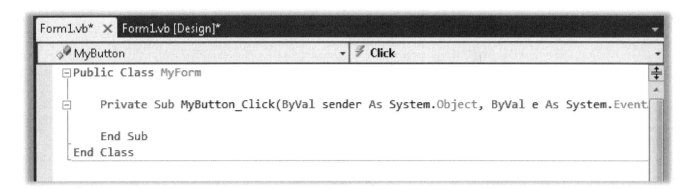

What you see is the code window for your form. The IDE has automatically created a function for you that will be run when the "MyButton" button is clicked. We will fill in the function with some code. Let's take a second and study this window. There are four lines of code. The first line just tells us that we are working on the code for the form named "MyForm". The code for this form stretches from the words "**Public Class** MyForm" to the last line, which says "**End Class**". These two statements are the bookends to our form.

The lines in the middle of the screen define the function which holds the code for your button. The two combo boxes at the top indicate this function will be run for "**MyButton**" whenever it receives a **Click** event. The function begins with the words "**Private Sub** MyButton_Click" and end with the line "**End Sub**". Between these two statements will go all the code for your button's click event function. When a user clicks on your button, the program will execute any statements that exist between these two lines. There are a number of things listed between the parenthesis ( ) after **MyButton_Click** that are for advanced purposes, so you can ignore them for now.

Of course, right now there are no statements in your click event, so let's add some! We are going to add code that will pop-up a message box that says "Hello, World!" To do this, we will use a special statement called **MsgBox**. **MsgBox** is a common Visual Basic function. We will talk more about functions and **MsgBox** in later chapters, but for now, we'll just cover some quick information. The **MsgBox** function looks like this:

```
MsgBox("Your text here.")
```

The first part of the above statement **MsgBox** just tells the program to call the **MsgBox**() function. The parentheses are used to enclose the parameters, or information that we are passing to this function. There is only one piece of information this function needs: the text to display in the message box. For our button, we will be displaying the text "Hello, World!" The text you want displayed should be surrounded by double quotation marks.

To add this code to our program, put your cursor on the line between "Public Sub" and "End Sub". Hit the Tab key to indent your new code slightly and then type the following line:

```
MsgBox("Hello, World!")
```

Something strange probably happened as soon as you typed in the first parenthesis. The IDE popped-up a "helper" window. This window contains helpful information about the function that you are using (in this case, info about **MsgBox**). The pop-up is a useful tool for programmers who need to know how to use a function. For now, however, just ignore the helper window and type in your line as shown above.

The resulting code window should look like this:

```
Form1.vb* X  Form1.vb [Design]*

MyButton                                      Click

Public Class Form1

    Private Sub MyButton_Click(ByVal sender As System.Object, ByVal e As System.EventArgs) Hand
        MsgBox("Hello, World!")
    End Sub
End Class
```

Now we are ready to test your program. Find the Start button (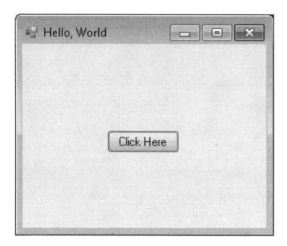) on the toolbar and click on it. Your program should show the form with the "Click Here" button.

Click on that button and you should see your message box!

You will notice that the title of your **MsgBox** is "Hello World2". Since we did not tell the program to use any specific title, the program just used the name of your program as the title.

Congratulations! You just wrote your first Visual Basic code statement!

 **Make sure you remember to save your project when you close the application. To do this, click on "File" and "Close Project". Name your project "Hello World2", make sure you are saving in your "C:\KidCoder\Windows Programming\My Projects" directory, and name your solution "Hello World2".**

Common Coding Mistakes

Now that you are writing code for your programs, let's go over some quick guidelines to avoid common coding problems.

One of the most common coding mishaps is accidentally clicking on your form and bringing up the code window. For example, let's say you are designing your form, and you accidentally double-click on the form itself. You would probably see a code window appear with the following code in it:

```
Public Class Form1

    Private Sub Form1_Load(ByVal sender As System.Object, ByVal e As System.EventArgs) Handles MyBase.Load

    End Sub
End Class
```

This simply means that the Visual Basic software thought you wanted to add some code that will run whenever the form first loads. If you make this type of mistake, don't panic! Just delete the code from the words "Private Sub" to "End Sub" and continue on with your project.

Another common coding mishap is when you receive an error that says "Handles clause requires a WithEvents variable…". This error is common when you have cut and pasted code into your code window without first designing your form. Let's say that we know we wanted to handle the "Click" event for a button in a program. We have similar code in another program, so we create a new project, go right to the code window and paste the code from our other program straight into the new project, like this:

```
Private Sub MyButton_Click(ByVal sender As System.Object, ByVal e As System.EventArgs) Handles Button1.Click

End Sub
```

As soon as you try to run the program you will see an error message. The cause of the error message is the word in the above image that is underlined with "squiggles". Since you have not yet added a button to the form (or if the button is not named "Button1"), the program does not know what to do with this code. It knows you want to handle a button named "Button1", but does not know where to find this particular control.

The best way to avoid this problem is to add your buttons and controls to the form (and give them meaningful names) before you ever try to add any code! If you need to fix the problem, either make sure you have a button named "**Button1**" on your form, or change the underlined "Button1" code to some other button name that is already on your form.

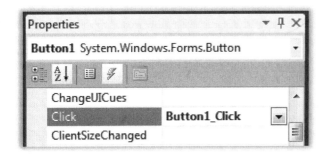

The button is linked to the click function on the Properties Sheet, so you can also fix problems from there! Click on your button in the Form Design window and look at the Properties Sheet. Click on the little lightning bolt icon (Events) to see a list of events and function handlers for that button.

Find the "Click" event and you can change the function name to match your code, or erase the function entirely. It is important to keep your form properties in sync with the code in your code window!

 **Chapter Review**

- An important element in Visual Basic is the Form, which represents a screen in the application.

- Controls are the graphical elements that can be placed onto a Form. These include buttons, text boxes, lists, pictures, etc.

- A programming language's *syntax* contains the rules about how a program can be written.

- An apostrophe (') is used in Visual Basic to start a comment line. Comments are non-code lines that are used to describe the program.

- There is no end-character to indicate the end of a statement in Visual Basic. The end of a statement is the end of the line.

- You can break a long statement across more than one line by adding an underscore (_) at the end.

- Visual Basic graphical programs are event-driven.

- Events are generated by user actions on controls.

- Events are handled by functions that you write.

- Make sure your event handler functions are properly linked to a control name on your form.

Your Turn: A Personal Message

In this activity you will practice creating message boxes using the **MsgBox**() function described in this chapter.

Open up the "Hello World2" project from this chapter. To do this, run the Visual Basic IDE and click on "File" and "Open Project". Your project should have been saved in "C:\KidCoder\Windows Programming\My Projects\Hello World2" and the filename should be "Hello World2.sln". Select this file to open the project. If you do not see your project's Form Design or code screens, use the icons in the Solution Explorer to display them.

Then add the following features to the program:

- Add another **MsgBox**() after the one in the program.
- Change the text in your new **MsgBox**() to display your name.

Now when you run your program you should see a second message box appear containing your name!

Chapter Four: Data Types and Variables

In this chapter you will learn how to name and store data within your program.

Lesson One: Data Types

Most useful programs require data to work. A calculator application needs numbers to calculate, an MP3 player needs music files to play, and an image editor needs pictures to load. In programming, data is carefully identified by its type. In this lesson we will cover some of the Visual Basic *data types* that we will use in this course.

Numeric Data

Numeric data types are very common. These types hold just what you think – numbers! There are several different kinds of numeric data types. Why not use just one numeric type? Because there are many different kinds of numbers: whole numbers, fractional numbers, large numbers and small numbers. You should choose the numeric data type that best matches what you need for your program. There are two general types of numeric data: *integer* and *fractional.*

Integers are positive or negative whole numbers. There are no fractions or decimal places in an integer value. Some examples of integer values are: a student's grade level (10), the number of books in a library (437), or a zip code (30004). You can add, subtract, multiply and divide an integer number.

Fractional numbers are real numbers, which are numbers that can contain an integer plus a fractional part, separated by a decimal point. Some examples of fractional values are: PI (3.14159), a student's grade point average (3.5), or the price of a t-shirt ($12.37). You don't have to have a fractional value in a decimal number...the digits to the right of the decimal point may all be zeros (4.00).

Both integers and fractional numbers can be stored in data types that use either more or less computer memory. The more memory a data type uses, the greater its possible range of values. Let's take a look at the specific types of integer and fractional data in Visual Basic.

Integer Types

Visual Basic defines several integer data types. The table below shows some common data types and the range of values they can hold.

Data Type	Possible Values
Byte	0 through 255
SByte	-128 through 127
Short	-32,768 through 32,767
Integer	-2,147,483,648 through 2,147,483,647
Long	-9,223,372,036,854,775,808 through 9,223,372,036,854,775,807

Fractional Types

The most common fractional data type is the **Double**. The **Double** variable holds very large or very small numbers with about 18 digits of precision. The largest possible **Double** is $1.79769313486231570 \times 10^{308}$.

The **Decimal** data type is also popular in Visual Basic. This data type holds fractional numbers with more decimal places than the **Double**. A **Decimal** number can contain 28 decimal places! However, using the **Decimal** type comes at a price: it takes more memory to store a very precise number. It's good practice to only use the data type that meets your program needs without taking up extra memory.

Character Data Types

Character data types store text information like names, descriptions, addresses, and titles. Character data is non-numeric...it cannot be added, subtracted, multiplied, or divided. There are two main character data types in Visual Basic: **Char** and **String**.

The **Char** data type is used to store a single character or letter. This is a great data type to use if you are going to store things like: letter grades "A" or "B", or one letter answers to questions, like "Y" for "yes" or "N" for "no".

If you want to store more than one letter at a time, you will need to use the **String** data type. A **String** can hold words or sentences, like names, addresses, or descriptions.

Constant Data Types

A piece of data that does not ever change is called "constant". The best example of a piece of constant data is the value of PI. We know that the value of PI is 3.14 and this value never ever changes. In order to protect this value from being accidentally changed while the program is running, we can declare the value as a **Constant**. Constant values cannot be changed once they are set in a program.

Other Data Types

There are other data types in the Visual Basic language. For instance, a **Boolean** data type holds either the value **True** or **False**. These are great for any part of your program that has to make a decision. You will be introduced to some other more complex data types as you progress through the course.

You may be tempted to use the largest possible data type for the data in your program. But remember, larger data types use more memory than the smaller types! It's good practice to use a data type just big enough to hold your expected data.

One last note on data types: if you use a data type incorrectly in a program, you could cause a "Runtime Error". This error will cause your program to stop in the middle of its execution. If, for instance, you tried to put the value "300" into a **Short** variable, you would cause an error, since a 300 is too great a number for the **Short** data type. You could also cause a runtime error if you attempt to assign a string value to a number variable or a number value to a string variable.

Always be aware of what data you are using in your program and pick your data types carefully!

Lesson Two: Variables

In addition to telling the program what kind of data type to use, we need to pick a name we will use to refer to the data in our program. When you create an instance of a data type and give it a name, that instance is called a *variable*. Variables are places where you store data in your program. You can change a variable's value while running the program (hence the name "variable").

Declaring a Variable

You create a variable in your program by *declaring* the variable. A variable declaration is just a way of telling Visual Basic that you will be expecting to use a specific type of data in your program. This is also a way of telling Visual Basic what name you will be calling this data. For instance, let's assume you wanted to write a program that asks a student for their current grade level. You would need a place to store the student's grade level in your program, so you might create a variable with a numeric data type that is named `GradeLevel`.

So how do we create a variable in Visual Basic? We use the following syntax:

```
Dim variableName As VariableType
```

Let's look at this statement in detail!

The first word is **Dim**. This stands for "dimension". Why "dimension"? Well, because that's the way it was in the original BASIC language and sometimes programmers have a hard time changing their habits! Nevertheless, every variable declaration starts with the keyword **Dim**. This *keyword* tells Visual Basic that we are about to create a new variable.

Keywords are words that have special meaning in a programming language. These words are often used to begin, end or enhance statements. Keywords are "reserved" for use by the language, which means that you cannot use them as a variable or function name.

The second word is "**variableName**". In a real variable declaration, this would be replaced with whatever name you want for your variable. It could be **gradeLevel**, **studentAge**, **address**, and so forth.

The third word is "**As**". This is also a keyword in Visual Basic and it just tells the program that we are about to announce what data type we will be using in this variable.

The last word is "**VariableType**". In a real variable declaration, this would be replaced with the data type you will be using. This could be: **Integer**, **Long**, **Short**, **Double**, **Decimal**, **Char**, **String**, or **Boolean**.

For example, a declaration for a variable that can hold a numeric grade level would look like this:

```
Dim gradeLevel As Integer
```

In this case, **gradeLevel** is our variable name and **Integer** is the data type.

You can declare more than one variable on the same line of code. All you have to do is separate the names of the variables with a comma. For instance, if we wanted to create a numeric variable for a student's grade level and a numeric variable for their age, we could do this:

```
Dim gradeLevel, studentAge As Integer
```

This creates two **Integer** variables at the same time: **gradeLevel** and **studentAge**.

Rules for Naming a Variable

You can name your variables almost anything you want. However, there are some rules to follow.

First, all names must be less than 256 characters long. Honestly, you will never need anywhere near this many characters. Typically a variable name should be short and sweet. Make your variable names mean something without making them really long!

Variable names must contain only alphabetic characters 'a' – 'z' or 'A' – 'Z', numbers '0' – '9', and underscores '_'. You may not begin a name with a number, only an alphabetic character or underscore. If you start with an underscore then you must have at least one other character in the name.

Variable names are often started with a lower-case letter, as in "**gradeLevel**". This is just a common convention among programmers but you may start with upper-case if you want.

A space is not allowed in your variable name. Visual Basic sees a space as the end of your variable name.

Here are some examples of some bad variable names:

123Number – Variable names cannot start with a number.

student.Name – You cannot have a period in a name.

my Address – You cannot have a space in a name.

In addition, the following kinds of variable names are allowed by the language, but should be discouraged:

ThisIsTheNumberVariableThatIWillBeUsing – This name is too long and not very informative.

myNumber – Even though we use this as an example in our lesson, it is not a very informative name either. We don't know what this "number" represents. Does it contain an address number or a sales total? It's best to be more descriptive.

Here are some examples of good variable names:

studentAddress
streetNumber
className

These variables do not have any restricted symbols or words and are all short, descriptive, and to-the-point. When you look at these variable names, you know exactly what data will be stored in them.

The names of constant variables are often created with all upper-case letters. This helps you to see the difference between a regular variable and a constant variable just by looking at the code.

Assigning Values to Variable

Now that we have picked what data type to use and we have declared our variable, how do we use it? Typically, you will want to assign a value to your variable. The assignment syntax looks like this:

```
variableName = Value
```

That's it! Pretty simple, right? The value that you assign can be anything from a mathematical expression (1+2), to a number (47), to a string ("Hello"), or a **Boolean** value ("**true**"). As long as you are assigning the correct type of data, and not trying to put "Hello" into an **Integer** variable, you will be fine.

Here is an example assigning a value to our **gradeLevel** integer variable:

```
gradeLevel = 6
```

Declaring and Assigning Constant Variables

A "constant" variable holds a value that cannot be changed. Here is an example:

```
Const STUDENT_ID As Integer = 123456
```

Notice that we use the keyword **Const** instead of the keyword **Dim** for a constant variable declaration. This tells the program that this is a value that cannot be changed while the program is running. You should also note that constant variables *must* be given a value when they are declared. This is the only time a value can be given to a variable of this type. It cannot be set or changed later in the program!

If you see an error message that variable "xyz" is not declared, then you are trying to use a variable name "xyz" that does not exist. Always make sure that you declare your variables BEFORE you try to use them!

Lesson Three: Using Data in Forms

In this lesson, we will be putting our new knowledge of variables to work! We are going to create a form that will use variables of different data types.

To begin, open the Visual Basic IDE and create a new project called "Data Types".

Change the **Name** and **Text** of "Form1" by clicking on the form and then finding the **(Name)** and **Text** properties in the Property Sheet. Change the **(Name)** property to "DataTypeForm" and the **Text** property to "Data Type Example".

We are going to create a program that uses several variables of different data types. We will use buttons and **MsgBoxes** to view our variables. Go ahead and create three buttons on your form. Change the **(Name)** on the first button to **NumericButton** and the **Text** to "Numeric Types". Change the **(Name)** on the second button to **CharButton** and the **Text** to "Character Types". Then change the **(Name)** on the third button to **BoolButton** and the **Text** to "Boolean Type".

Your form should look something like this:

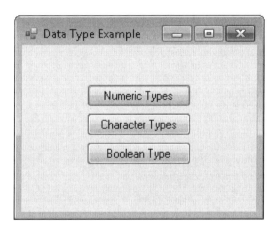

Now double-click on the "Numeric Types" button to bring up the code window. You should see a newly created event handler function for the button similar to this:

```
Private Sub NumericButton_Click(......
End Sub
```

We are going to add our numeric data variables between the line "Private Sub" and the line "End Sub". We will create two numeric variables: a **Long** and an **Integer**. Now, type in two variable declarations like this:

```
Dim longNumber As Long
Dim integerNumber As Integer
```

Next, add the following statements to assign values to our variables, making sure to put the right kind of data into each type:

```
longNumber = 1234567890
integerNumber = 1234
```

Now let's create pop-ups using the **MsgBox()** function that will display the values in our variables!

The ampersand character (&) is used to convert a numeric value to a string and glue it to another string. We want to display the values of **longNumber** and **integerNumber** as text within the message. We will talk more about this special character in a later lesson. Type in these two **MsgBox** statements:

```
MsgBox("longNumber: " & longNumber)
MsgBox("integerNumber: " & integerNumber)
```

Your completed code should look like the function below:

```
Private Sub NumericButton_Click(ByVal sender As System.Object, _
                                ByVal e As System.EventArgs) _
                                Handles NumericButton.Click
    Dim longNumber As Long
    Dim integerNumber As Integer

    longNumber = 1234567890
    integerNumber = 1234
    MsgBox("longNumber: " & longNumber)
    MsgBox("integerNumber: " & integerNumber)
End Sub
```

Go ahead and run your program, and try out the Numeric Button. Did you see the expected messages? Feel free to change the numbers around too!

Now let's add some code to our "Character Types" button. Double-click on the "Character Types" button to open up the code window. You should see the event handler function for that button:

```
Private Sub CharButton_Click(......

End Sub
```

We will add our character variables between the "Private Sub" line and the "End Sub" line. Start by creating a **Char** and a **String** variable using the following code:

```
Dim myChar As Char
Dim myString As String
```

Now assign a value to these variables by typing in these two statements:

```
myChar = "A"
myString = "This is my string"
```

Finally, create some **MsgBoxes** to display the values of our variables:

```
MsgBox("myChar: " & myChar)
MsgBox("myString: " & myString)
```

Notice the use of the special "&" character again to glue two pieces of text together.

Your completed code should look similar to this:

```
Private Sub CharButton_Click(ByVal sender As System.Object, _
                             ByVal e As System.EventArgs) _
                             Handles CharButton.Click
    Dim myChar As Char
    Dim myString As String

    myChar = "A"
    myString = "This is my string"

    MsgBox("myChar: " & myChar)
    MsgBox("myString: " & myString)
End Sub
```

Go ahead and run your program to test this button. Feel free to change the text in your variables and experiment with the output!

Now let's add some code to the final button, "Boolean Button". Double-click the Boolean Button to bring up the code window. You should see your event handler function for that button:

```
Private Sub BoolButton_Click(......

End Sub
```

Once again, we will add our code between the lines: "Private Sub" and "End Sub". Create one **Boolean** variable with the following declaration:

```
     Dim myBoolean As Boolean
```

Then assign a value to this variable. The possible values for a **Boolean** are either **True** or **False**:

```
    myBoolean = True
```

Finally, create a **MsgBox()** to display our **Boolean** variable:

```
    MsgBox("myBoolean: " & myBoolean)
```

The completed code should look like this:

```
    Private Sub BoolButton_Click(ByVal sender As System.Object, _
                           ByVal e As System.EventArgs) _
                           Handles BoolButton.Click
        Dim myBoolean As Boolean
        myBoolean = True

        MsgBox("myBoolean: " & myBoolean)
    End Sub
```

That's it! You should be able to run your program and test all three buttons! Try changing the Boolean assignment to **False** and observe the output.

Remember to save your project when you close the IDE. To do this, click on "File" and "Close Project". Name your project "Data Types", make sure you are saving in your "C:\KidCoder\Windows Programming\My Projects" directory, and name your solution "Data Types".

 **Chapter Review**

- Most useful programs require some sort of data to work.

- Numeric data types are common data types that store numbers.

- There are two categories of numeric data types: integer and fractional.

- **Short**, **Integer**, and **Long** data types all hold integer numbers of different sizes.

- **Double** and **Decimal** hold fractional numbers with different precision and ranges.

- There are two main character data types: **Char**, for single characters, and **String**, for one or more characters.

- When you create an instance of a data type and give it name, that instance is called a *variable*.

- When naming your variable you must follow the Visual Basic variable naming rules.

- Assigning a value to a variable is as easy as using an equals sign: variableName = Value.

- You can use the ampersand character (&) to glue together two strings into a larger string.

Your Turn: Various Variables

In this activity, you will create some more variables with different data types.

Open up the "Data Types" project from this chapter. To do this, run the Visual Basic IDE and click on "File" and "Open Project". Your project should have been saved in "C:\KidCoder\Windows Programming\My Projects\Data Types" and the filename should be "Data Types.sln". Select this file to open the project. If you do not see your project's screen and code, use the icons in the Solution Explorer to display them.

Now add some new things to your program:

- Double-click on the "Numeric" button and add code to do the following:
    o Add a **Decimal** variable called **decimalNumber**
    o Assign a value to **decimalNumber** (you choose!)

- Add a **MsgBox**() command to display the value of **decimalNumber**

When you run your modified program you should now see a new pop-up when you click the Numeric button that shows your decimal value. Here is an example:

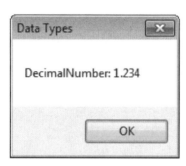

Chapter Five: Basic Flow Control

In this chapter you will learn how to test variables against certain conditions, and then make decisions in your program based on the results.

Lesson One: Expressions and Operators

Expressions are parts of a statement that combine one, two, or more numbers or variables together. The result may be another number or a **Boolean True** or **False**.

Math Expressions vs. Logical Expressions

A math expression is a mathematical statement that always results in a number. For example, the following statement is a mathematical expression, because it results in the number 3:

```
1 + 2
```

The following expressions are all math expressions:

```
4 - 3
5 * 2 + 12
3.14159 / 32.1
```

A logical expression looks somewhat like a math expression, but it uses *relational* or *conditional operators* to always evaluate to either **True** or **False**. A logical expression can never result in a number. For example, the following statement is a logical expression:

```
age > 10
```

This expression will either be **True** or **False** depending on whether or not the **age** variable is indeed greater than 10. The following expressions are logical expressions:

```
4 < 3
5 < (2 + 3)
```

Logical expressions are very important in programming, because they allow your program to make decisions about what code to run. For instance, let's say we had a list of student names and we only wanted to print out those student who were older than 10. We would use a logical expression (age > 10) to decide whether or not to print each student's name. This type of decision in a program is often called *flow control*, since the result of the expression will decide which statements the program executes.

 **A math expression will always result in a number. A logical expression will always result in either True or False. A logical expression cannot result in a number, and a math expression cannot result in True or False!**

Conditional Operators

All logical expressions involving two or more components require a *conditional operator*. These are the comparison symbols that are used in logical expressions. Let's look at some common operators!

The first conditional operator is the *equal to* (=) operator. The result of this operator is **True** if both sides of a logical expression are the same. For example:

```
1 = 2     is a false statement since 1 does not equal 2.
2 = 1     is a false statement since 2 does not equal 1.
1 = 1     is a true statement since 1 equals 1.
```

The next conditional operator is the *not equal to* (<>) operator. This result of this operator in a logical expression returns **True** if the two sides of the expression are not equal to each other. The result is **False** if they are equal to each other. For example:

```
1 <> 2     is a true statement since 1 is not equal to 2.
2 <> 1     is a true statement since 2 is not equal to 1.
1 <> 1     is a false statement since 1 is equal to 1.
```

Next, we have the *less than* (<) operator. The result of this operator is **True** if the left side of the expression is smaller, or less than the right side. The statement is **False** if the left side of the equation is not less than the right side. For example:

```
1 < 2     is a true statement since 1 is less than 2.
2 < 1     is a false statement since 2 is not less than 1.
1 < 1     is a false statement since 1 is not less than 1.
```

The next operator is the *greater than* (>) operator. The result of this operator in a logical expression is **True** if the left side of an expression is larger than right side. The result is **False** if the left side is not greater than the right side. For example:

```
1 > 2        is a false statement since 1 is not greater than 2.
2 > 1        is a true statement since 2 is greater than 1.
1 > 1        is a false statement since 1 is not greater than 1.
```

The next conditional operator is the *less than or equal to* (<=) operator. The result of this operator in a logical expression is **True** if the left side of an expression is smaller than or equal to the right side. The result is **False** if the left side is not smaller or equal to the right side. For example:

```
1 <= 2       is a true statement since 1 is less than 2.
2 <= 1       is false since 2 isn't less than nor equal to 1.
1 <= 1       is a true statement since 1 is equal to 1.
```

Finally, we have the *greater than or equal to* (>=) operator. The result of this operator in a logical expression is **True** if the left side of an expression is larger than or equal to the right side. The result is **False** if the left side is not larger than or equal to the right side. For example:

```
1 >= 2       is false since 1 isn't greater than nor equal to 2
2 >= 1       is a true statement since 2 is greater than 1.
1 >= 1       is a true statement since 1 is equal to 1.
```

These conditional operators are very important in determining flow control, since they help the program to make decisions about what statements to execute.

Logical Operators

You may use the logical operators "**And**" and "**Or**" to join together two or more logical expressions. The resulting larger expression still evaluates to **True** or **False**

When using the **And** operator, if both logical expressions are **True** then the result is **True**. If either (or both) of the logical expressions are **False** then the result is **False**.

Let's go back to our student list example. If we want to print out a list of students that are over the age of 10, and are named "Bob", we could write the following expression:

```
(age > 10) And (name = "Bob")
```

The logical expression above will evaluate to **True** if both **age** is greater than 10 **And name** is equal to "**Bob**".

When using the **Or** operator, if either logical expression is **True** then the result is **True**. If both of the logical expressions are **False** then the result is **False**.

Continuing our student example, this logical expression would be true for all students that are 10 or 11 years old:

```
(age = 10) Or (age = 11)
```

Another useful logical operator is the **Not** operator. This operator will change a **Boolean** value from **False** to **True** or **True** to **False**. Here is an example expression that will be true for all students that are not 12 years old:

```
Not (age = 12)
```

Variables in Logical Expressions

Any of the simple numbers we demonstrated above when talking about expressions can be replaced by variables instead. All of the basic numeric variable types can be used freely in logical expressions. For example, if **age** was a numeric data type, these expressions are valid:

```
age > 18
age = 18
age <> 18
```

You can also use conditional operators to compare strings.

```
name = "Barney"
name <> "Wilma"
```

This will only compare exact strings. If we compared the string "Barney" and "barney", the result would be **False**, since the case of the letter "b" is different in each string. We will discuss some better ways to compare strings in a later chapter.

 Notice that the equals sign is used to do two main things in Visual Basic: assign value "a=3" and compare values "if (age = 10)". Visual Basic will simply look at the context of your program to determine whether to assign or compare a value. You should always make sure that you are using the equals sign correctly in your program.

Lesson Two: The "If" Statement

Now that we understand how to build logical expressions that evaluate to **True** or **False**, let's look at how we can use them in a program to select which statements to execute.

The If() Statement

The **If()** statement tests a logical expression and executes some statements if the expression evaluates to **True**. The **If()** syntax looks like this:

```
If (logical expression) Then
      ' execute these statement(s) if the logical expression is true
End If
```

Let's look at these statements word-by-word. The first line starts with the **If** keyword. This keyword tells the program that we are about to make a decision.

The second part is "(logical expression)". This is where we will put our logical expression, like "age > 10".

The next word is the **Then** keyword. This keyword tells the program that if our expression is **True**, *then* we will execute the following statements.

The next line(s) contains any statements that we want to execute if our condition is **True**. If we wanted to display the names of students whose age is > 10, we would put our display statements here.

The last line is the **End If** statement. This tells the program that we have finished our block of statements to execute if the logical expression was **True**. If the logical expression was **True** the program would flow to the **Then** block of statements and from there continue with the next statement following the **End If**. If the logical expression was **False** then the program flow would skip all of the statements in the **Then** block and continue with the next statement following the **End If**.

Here is a sample **If()** statement that determines a student's letter grade based on a score:

```
If (studentGrade > 90) Then
      letterGrade = "A"
End If
```

The Else Statement

The **If()** statement is very simple and effective. But what if we want to do one thing if our expression is **True**, and another if it is **False**? To do this, we need to add the **Else** keyword:

```
If (logical expression) Then
        ' execute these statement(s) if the logical expression is true
Else
        ' execute these statement(s) if the logical expression is false
End If
```

The first part in our **If()** statement is still the same. This is our test for our logical expression. The next line(s) still hold the statements that will run if our logical expression is **True**. The third line is where our new **Else** keyword is located. The next line(s) following the **Else** statement are the statements that will execute if our logical expression is **False**. The last line is still the **End If** statement, which tells the program that we are done with our **If()** statement.

```
If (studentGrade > 90) Then
        letterGrade = "A"
Else
        letterGrade = "B"
End If
```

The "ElseIf" Statement

There is one last kind of **If()** statement that uses the **ElseIf** keyword. This is used if you want to test more than one logical expression in series. For instance, let's say we have a variable that has a person's age in it. We may want to do one thing only if they are less than 10 years old, and another thing if they are less than 20, and nothing at all if they are 20 or more. Our example might be written as follows:

```
If (age < 10) Then
        ' execute these statements if less than 10
ElseIf age < 20
        ' execute these statements if greater than or equal to 10 but
        ' less than 20
End If
```

We are using the **ElseIf** keyword to add another logical expression that will be tested *only* if the first logical expression evaluated to **False**. This means for this example that we will perform a specific action if the student is less than 10 years old, or a different action if the student is less than 20 years old, or nothing at all if the student is 20 or more years old.

Let's expand our grading example to assign a few different letter grades based on the student's score.

```
If (studentGrade > 90) Then
        letterGrade = "A"

ElseIf (studentGrade > 80) Then
        letterGrade = "B"

ElseIf (studentGrade > 70) Then
        letterGrade = "C"
End If
```

Lesson Three: Using the "If" Statement

Now that we have learned about logical expressions and **If()** statements, let's see them in action! In this lesson, we are going to create a program that will display some descriptive text regarding the current time.

Go ahead and open up the Visual Basic IDE. Once it's open, create a new project called "If Statements". Click on the form and change the **(Name)** property to "ClockForm" and the **Text** property to "My Clock"

Next add a button to the form. The user will click this button to see the current time. Once you add the button, change its **(Name)** to "TimeButton" and its **Text** to "Current Time".

Your form should now look like this:

Now we will add some code to our button. Double-click on the "Current Time" button to bring up the code window.

Add two lines of code in your button click function that will declare a variable called **currentTime** and assign to it the current time.

```
Dim currentTime As DateTime
currentTime = DateTime.Now
```

Here we have declared a variable named **currentTime** of the type **DateTime**. This special data type is part of Visual Basic and can hold a date and time value. This is our first example where a variable contains something more than a simple number, string, or Boolean! The second line sets the value of our new variable to the current date and time by using the special command "**DateTime.Now**".

Now we could just send a **MsgBox()** to the user with the current time and date, but what fun would that be? Let's jazz it up a little with a greeting that includes either "Good morning", "Good afternoon", or "Good night". In order to do that, we need to know if it is morning, afternoon, or night. We will use an **If()** statement to figure out what message to send our user.

The current hour in our **currentTime** variable is a 24-hour value, like military time. So, 11am is represented by the hour "11", 4pm would be the hour "16", etc. This makes it easy for us to figure out if the current time is morning, afternoon, or night.

The first thing we need to do in our program is retrieve the current hour. This is done by accessing the **Hour** property of **currentTime**. We will use an **Integer** variable called "**iHour**" to store this value. Add the following lines to your program:

```
Dim iHour As Integer
iHour = currentTime.Hour
```

The goal for our **If()** statement will be to determine:

> If the current hour is less than 12, it must be morning.
> If the current hour is more than 12, but less than 18 (6pm), it must be afternoon.
> If the current hour is more than 18 (6pm), it must be night.

Now begin the **If()** statement by checking to see if it's morning time:

```
If (iHour < 12) Then
        MsgBox("Good Morning! The time is now: " & currentTime)
```

If the current hour is less than 12 (noon), then it must be morning, so we send a "Good Morning" message to the user. By adding the value of **currentTime** to the message, we will also show the user the current time on their computer.

If the current hour is not less than 12, then we need to send either a "Good afternoon" or "Good evening" message. Add this **ElseIf** statement to see if it's afternoon time:

```
ElseIf (iHour < 18) Then
        MsgBox("Good Afternoon! The time is now: " & currentTime)
```

Here we use a logical expression to see if the current time is less than 18 (6pm). Remember, if this condition is tested then we know the hour is already greater than or equal to 12 because the first **If()** condition was **False**.

Finally, you should use an **Else** statement to handle evening time. If the hour is not less than 12, and it is also not less than 18, then it must be greater than or equal to 18 (6pm). In this case, we send our evening message.

```
Else
        MsgBox("Good Evening! The time is now: " & currentTime)
End If
```

Note that the **Else** statement will only execute its statements if *none* of the other logical expressions evaluated as **True**. As always, you need to make sure your **If** statement ends with the line **End If**. The Visual Basic IDE will probably put this in for you, but you should always check to make sure.

Your final "**TimeButton_Click()**" function should look like this:

```
Private Sub TimeButton_Click(ByVal sender As System.Object, _
                        ByVal e As System.EventArgs) Handles TimeButton.Click

    Dim currentTime As DateTime
    Dim iHour As Integer

    currentTime = DateTime.Now
    iHour = currentTime.Hour

    If (iHour < 12) Then
        MsgBox("Good Morning! The time is now: " & currentTime)

    ElseIf (iHour < 18) Then
        MsgBox("Good Afternoon! The time is now: " & currentTime)

    Else
        MsgBox("Good Evening! The time is now: " & currentTime)
    End If
End Sub
```

That's it! Run your program and test it out!

Here is an example message box:

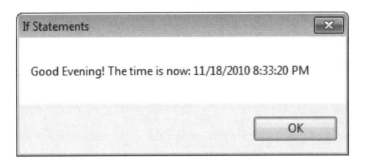

 Make sure you remember to save your project when you close the application. To do this, click on "File" and "Close Project". Name your project "If Statements", make sure you are saving in your "C:\KidCoder\Windows Programming\My Projects" directory, and name your solution "If Statements".

 **Chapter Review**

- Math expressions will always result in a number

- Logical expressions will always result in either **True** or **False**.

- Conditional operators =, <>, <, >, <=, and >= are used in logical expressions to compare values.

- Logical operators **And** and **Or** can be used to join one or more logical expressions to make a larger expression. In a typical program, a logical expression will contain at least one variable.

- The **Not** logical operator will change a Boolean value from **True** to **False** or **False** to **True**.

- **If()** statements use logical expressions to make decisions in a program. If the logical expression is **True** then a specific set of statements will be executed.

- The **Else** keyword in an **If()** statement allows a program to perform an action if the logical expression **False**.

- The **Else If** keywords in an **If()** expression allows a program to make multiple decisions based on one or more logical expressions.

Your Turn: Weekend Dreaming

In this activity, you will add another **If()** statement to check and see if the current day is a weekday or a weekend day and display a corresponding message to the user with a **MsgBox()**.

To do this, you will use the **DayOfWeek** property of a **DateTime** variable (`currentTime` in our program). This property is very similar to the **Hour** property that we used in the lesson. The **DayOfWeek** property will give you a numeric representation of the day of the week. Sunday is 0, Monday is 1, Tuesday is 2, and so on.

Load the "If Statements" project from this chapter. To do this, open up the Visual Basic IDE and click on "File" and "Open Project". Your project should have been saved in "C:\KidCoder\Windows Programming\My Projects\If Statements" and the filename should be "If Statements.sln". Go ahead and open this project. If you do not see your project's screen and code, use the icons in the Solution Explorer to display the frames.

Now add to your program as follows:

- Add a variable to hold the numeric value of the **currentTime.DayofWeek** property.
- Add an **If()** statement to see if the current day of the week is a weekend day (a value 0 or 6) or a weekday (any other value). Send out a message to the user with a **MsgBox()** to tell them whether this is or is not a weekend day.

When you run your program on a weekday, you should see your message stating that it is a weekday. When you run the program on a weekend you should see your weekend message. Here's an example:

Chapter Six: Getting User Input

This chapter will explain how to ask for, receive, and validate user input in your program.

Lesson One: InputBoxes

So far we have used the Visual Basic **MsgBox**() pop-up window to display output to the user. In this lesson, we will learn how to use the **InputBox**() pop-up window to receive input.

The **InputBox**() in Visual Basic is a special function which can be used to get a single line of input text from a user. For example, if you needed to know a user's age, or you needed to know their home state, you could use an **InputBox**().

When you use the **InputBox**() function, the program will show a simple window with a question for the user, which you provide. The window will also have a place for the user to type in their answer, an "OK" button and a "Cancel" button. If the user clicks the OK button, any information typed into the text box will be sent back to your program. If the user clicks the Cancel button, they will return to your program without sending any information.

Here is what the **InputBox**() syntax looks like:

```
stringVariable = InputBox("question for user", "title for window")
```

Let's look at this statement one part at a time:

The first **stringVariable** is the name of some **String** variable that you must have already declared. When the user clicks the OK button, Visual Basic will put their answer into this variable. If the user clicks the Cancel button, this variable will contain an empty string.

The next part is the **InputBox**() keyword. This just tells Visual Basic that we will be showing an input box pop-up window.

The items within the parentheses are the parameters for our **InputBox**(). These parameters help us to customize the **InputBox**() so that it looks just like we want it to. The first parameter, "question for user", is just a string that tells the user what information we will need. For example, if we need to ask the user what their home state is, we could use the string: "Please enter your home state:"

The second parameter, "title for window", allows us to give our **InputBox**() a useful caption. Continuing the example above, we might use "Home State Question" as our title.

Now let's look at a complete example to ask a question about the user's home state:

```
Dim homeState As String
homeState = InputBox("Please enter your home State: ", _
                     "Home State Question")
```

When run, the **InputBox**() pop-up window would look like this:

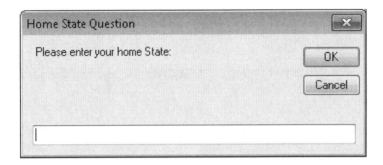

Simple, yet powerful!

 There are many more parameters available for the InputBox() function. For this course, we will only be using the two parameters mentioned above. If you are interested in learning about the other parameters, just look up the InputBox() function in your MSDN help library.

Lesson Two: Getting User Input from Forms

The **InputBox()** function is a quick and simple way to get a single piece of information from a user. But what if you need more than one piece of information? What if you need to get a person's whole address and not just their home state? For this, you would want to create a custom form that has several textboxes for users to enter information. In addition, your form would need to have an OK button to indicate when the user is finished.

Let's walk through the creation and use of a custom form together. Open up the Microsoft Visual Basic IDE and create a new project called "User Input".

Once you have created your project, we need to rename and title our form. Click on the form and then look at the Property Sheet. Find the property called **(Name)** and change it from "Form1" to "MyInputForm". Then find the property called **Text** and change it from "Form1" to "Address Form".

Now, take a look at your blank form and the Controls Toolbar. For our address form, we will need four pieces of information from our user: their street address, city, state and zip code. We will be using four textboxes where the user can enter their information and four labels, so they know which information goes into each textbox. Go ahead and drag and drop four labels and four textboxes onto your form.

You will need to line up your labels with your textboxes. The end result should look like the form shown on the right.

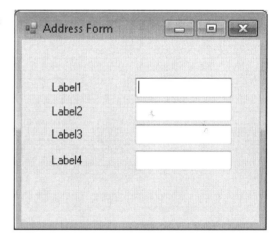

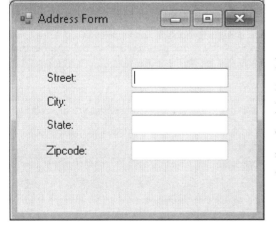

Next we need to give our labels and textboxes more meaningful names or text than Label1, Label2, etc. Click on Label1 and then look at the Property Sheet. Find the property called **Text** and change the text from "Label1" to "Street:" Then click on Label2 and do the same thing to change the text from "Label2" to "City:" Next, change the text for Label3 to "State:", and the text for Label4 to "Zip code:". Your new form is shown on the left.

We will also need to change the name of our textboxes. To do this, click on the first textbox and find the property called **(Name)** in the Property Sheet. Change the name from "Textbox1" to "StreetTextbox". Then click on the second textbox and do the same thing to change the name from "Textbox2" to "CityTextbox". Next, change the name for Textbox3 to "StateTextbox" and the name for "Textbox4" to "ZipTextbox".

Now we need to add an OK button to our form. Drag and drop a button onto your form and put it at the bottom of the screen. Your form should look as shown on the right.

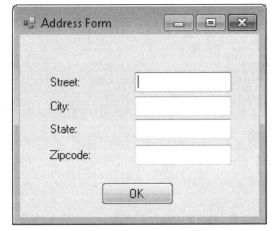

Next let's rename and change the text for this button. Click on "Button1" and then look at the Property Sheet. Change the **(Name)** property from "Button1" to "OKButton" and the "Text" property from "Button1" to "OK". Your final form is shown on the left.

Great! Now we have our form which will ask our user for their full address information. Now let's talk about how we are going to retrieve that information when the user clicks the "OK" button.

Retrieving information from textboxes is easy! Once the user clicks the OK button, we will just look at each textbox's **Text** property to see what they have entered. For this example, we will use this information in a pop-up window showing user what information they typed onto the fields.

Now double-click on the "OK" Button to create our click event. You should now see the code window with the following event handler function:

```vb
Public Class MyInputForm
        Private Sub OKButton_Click(ByVal sender As System.Object, _
                    ByVal e As System.EventArgs) Handles OKButton.Click
        End Sub
End Class
```

We are going to add our new code inside the button click handler function.

First, declare new **String** variables to hold the address data. Place your cursor within the function (after the "Private Sub..." line) and create four **String** variables:

```
Dim streetString As String
Dim cityString As String
Dim stateString As String
Dim zipString As String
```

Now we have created the strings which will hold our user's data. But how do we get the data into these strings? In order to get the information from the textboxes, we will read the **Text** property of each textbox. Each textbox can be referred to by the name property we gave it on the form. To read a property of the text box (e.g. the **Text** value), use the name of the text box, a period, and then the property name. Here how we can retrieve the information from the four textboxes we named on our form:

```
streetString = StreetTextbox.Text
cityString = CityTextbox.Text
stateString = StateTextbox.Text
zipString = ZipTextbox.Text
```

Notice how we set our **String** variables equal to the name of each textbox with a ".**Text**" afterwards. This tells our program to take the text that is currently in that textbox and place it into our **String** variable.

Your code so far should look something like this:

```
Private Sub OKButton_Click(ByVal sender As System.Object, _
                    ByVal e As System.EventArgs) _
                    Handles OKButton.Click
    Dim streetString As String
    Dim cityString As String
    Dim stateString As String
    Dim zipString As String

    streetString = StreetTextbox.Text
    cityString = CityTextbox.Text
    stateString = StateTextbox.Text
    zipString = ZipTextbox.Text
End Sub
```

83

Now that's all fine and dandy, but what will we do with the information? Let's toss it into a **MsgBox()** to show the user what they entered. To do this, we will enter one more statement to call the **MsgBox()** function, combining all of the input strings into a single message:

```
MsgBox("You entered: " & streetString & " " & cityString & " " & _
                stateString & " " & zipString)
```

Notice the use of the ampersand (&) character. This is used to combine our strings together into one big string. Also, note that we used an underscore (_) at the end of our line. This is necessary if your statement will take more than one line. If you fit the whole statement on one line, you do not need this character.

Also notice that we added a space between each string in order to separate the varaible data in the displayed message. Now your final OK Button code should look like this:

```
Private Sub OKButton_Click(ByVal sender As System.Object, _
                ByVal e As System.EventArgs) _
                Handles OKButton.Click
    Dim streetString As String
    Dim cityString As String
    Dim stateString As String
    Dim zipString As String

    streetString = StreetTextbox.Text
    cityString = CityTextbox.Text
    stateString = StateTextbox.Text
    zipString = ZipTextbox.Text

    MsgBox("You entered: "& streetString & " " & cityString & " " & _
            stateString & " " & zipString)
End Sub
```

Now let's run the program and see what it looks like!

Type in some data for all 4 fields and click the OK button.

Your popup should display this formatted text!

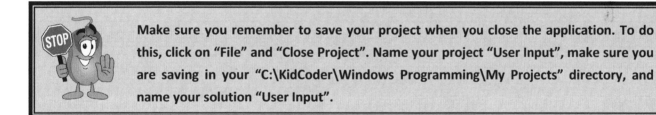

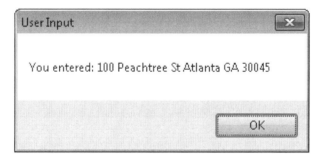 Make sure you remember to save your project when you close the application. To do this, click on "File" and "Close Project". Name your project "User Input", make sure you are saving in your "C:\KidCoder\Windows Programming\My Projects" directory, and name your solution "User Input".

Lesson Three: Validating User Input

The last lesson on user input is about input *validation*. Validation is where you make sure the input that the user entered matches what you expected them to provide. For instance, let's say you ask the user for two numbers to add together. You will want to make sure the user gives you numbers and not letters. You cannot add "A" and "B"!

There is always a chance that a user will enter invalid or incomplete data or even no data at all! You should always check to make sure the data is what you expect before you use it in your program. So how do we do this? There are a few simple functions in Visual Basic that will help us out.

The first helper is a function called **IsNumeric**(). This function does just what it says: it checks a string to make sure all characters are numeric characters. It will return **True** if all characters are numeric, or **False** if there are any non-numeric characters.

Here is an example that will perform some calculations if an input string is purely numeric.

```
If (  IsNumeric(myUserString)  ) Then
        ' do some calculations here
End If
```

So, if we wanted to display an error if the zip code in our address example was not numeric, we could use this logic:

```
If (  Not IsNumeric(ZipTextbox.Text)  ) Then
        MsgBox("Zip code must be all numbers")
End If
```

Another possible scenario is that the user did not enter anything at all. To check for this condition, we would simply check for the empty string " " (two quotation marks in a row). If we wanted to make sure that the user entered a street address, our validation check would have looked like this:

```
If (streetTextbox.Text = "") Then
        MsgBox ("You must enter a street value!")
End If
```

If the textbox is empty, then the user has not entered a street address!

Another type of validation will ensure the user entered a value that is within the range we need to use in our program. For instance, in our address example, we would want to make sure that our zip code is a 5-digit positive number. We can convert the textbox string contents to a numeric value using the **Val()** function:

```
If ((Val(ZipTextbox.Text) < 10000) Or _
        (Val(ZipTextbox.Text) > 99999)) _
Then
        MsgBox("You must enter a 5-digit zip code!")
End If
```

The **Val()** function returns an integer which we can then check to see if the number is in a 5-digit range.

Chapter Review

- An **InputBox()** is a great way to quickly and easily get a single piece of information from a user.

- To get more than one piece of information from a user, you will need to create a custom form.

- To get the string that a user has entered into a Textbox on a form, just use the textbox name and the **.Text** property in your program code.

- Validating user input enables a programmer to make sure that the data that is entered by the user is the right type of data for the program.

- The **IsNumeric()** function will tell you if a string contains only numeric digits.

- The **Val()** function will convert a string to a number.

- You can use the **IsNumeric()** and **Val()** functions to help to make sure that string inputs are fully numeric and the right range of numbers.

- To see if a user has left a Textbox blank, just check to see if the **.Text** property is equal to " ".

Your Turn: Enter Your Name, Please.

In this activity, we will add a name field to our "User Input" project.

Open up the "User Input" project from this chapter. To do this, open up the Visual Basic IDE and click on "File" and "Open Project". Your project should have been saved in "C:\KidCoder\Windows Programming\User Input" and the filename should be "User Input.sln". Select this file to open the project.

Now try and add the following to the form:

- A textbox where the user can enter their name
- A label which tells the user what information to enter into the new textbox. (e.g.: "Enter your name:")
- Make sure the user enters some information in the new Name textbox. If they leave it blank, use a **MsgBox()** to tell them that they have left that field blank.
- In the code for the OK button, add the name information to the **MsgBox()** output string.

When run, your program should now add the user's name to the output pop-up window, or display an error message if the name field was left blank.

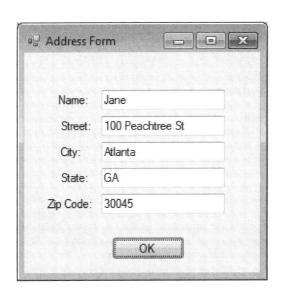

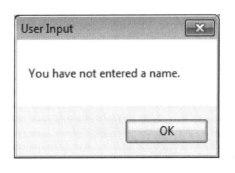

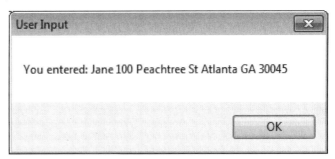

Chapter Seven: Working with Numbers

This chapter will describe how to convert between numeric and string data types, and how to perform common math operations on numeric data.

Lesson One: Converting Between Numbers and Strings

Sometimes your programs will need to convert a value from a number to a string or from a string to a number. In Visual Basic, these conversions are done with some handy built-in functions.

Numbers to Strings

Let's say you are creating a program that prints out the number of books in a library. The number of books is most likely stored in a numeric variable, but you need to print the number in a string like "We have 92 books on space flights." The number 92 needs to be converted to the string "92" in order to be printed.

In order to convert a number to a string, we use the **Str()** function. This function is extremely simple: it takes a number value as a parameter and returns a string value. Here is what this function looks like:

```
Dim stringValue As String = Str(numberValue)
```

As you expect, **stringValue** is the **String** variable that will hold the converted number. The **Str()** function name is next, followed by the one and only parameter: **numberValue**, which should be an **Integer**. This function is very easy to use!

Strings to Numbers

In another program it may be necessary to convert a string into a number. If you ask a user to enter a number into an **InputBox()**, for example, the **InputBox()** will return the number that they enter as a string. If you want to perform any math on this data, you will first need to convert it to a number.

In this case, you will need to use the **Val()** function. This function is the opposite of **Str()**; it takes a string value as a parameter and returns a number. Here is what this function looks like:

```
Dim numberValue As Integer = Val(stringValue)
```

The **numberValue** is the integer variable that will hold the converted number. The **Val()** function name is next, followed by the only parameter: **stringValue**, which is the string that you want to convert into a number.

This function is also easy to use, but you should be sure that the string you are converting contains numbers and not other characters. One way to do this is to use the **IsNumeric()** function first! **IsNumeric()** will return **True** if the entire string contains only numbers, or **False** if any non-numeric characters are found.

```
If (IsNumeric(stringValue)) Then
        numberValue = Val(stringValue)
End If
```

Here we first checked to see if the input string value contained all numbers and only then did we use the **Val()** function to convert the string to a number.

Lesson Two: Math operators (+, -. *, /) and Common Functions

In this lesson we will learn how to perform basic math operations on numeric data.

Defining the Operators

Math operators are the symbols that we use to do mathematical calculations, like adding, subtracting, multiplying and dividing. Visual Basic (and just about every other programming language) uses these special characters to perform the math operations:

+	Addition
-	Subtraction
*	Multiplication
/	Division

The plus sign ("+") is used to add two values together. An addition expression can be formed like this, where **Number1** and **Number2** can be any two numeric variables or hard-coded numbers:

```
Number1 + Number2
```

The minus sign ("-") is used to subtract one value from another value. A subtraction expression can be formed like this:

```
Number1 - Number2
```

The asterisk ("*****") character is used to multiply two values together. Here is a multiplication expression:

```
Number1 * Number2
```

The forward slash ("**/**") is used to divide one value with another value. The left number is the dividend (number that gets divided) and the right number is the divisor (number that is doing the division):

```
Number1 / Number2
```

Make sure when dividing that you never use 0, or a variable containing 0, as the second number. You can't divide by zero; this will cause a program error!

How to Use Math Operators

In a program, you can combine math operators and numeric parameters to form an arithmetic expression. The results of that expression can then be assigned to a numeric variable:

```
myInteger = 3 + 4
```

In your arithmetic expressions, any or all of the numeric operands can of course be variables:

```
myInteger = firstInteger + secondInteger
```

You can also use arithmetic expressions as part of larger logical expressions:

```
If ((input * 10) < maxResult) Then
        ' more logic here
End If
```

Standard Visual Basic Math Functions

There are several standard Visual Basic math functions that you can use in your programs. It's much easier to use pre-built functions to perform these tasks instead of writing your own functions or repeating lots of common code throughout your program.

The first math function we will discuss is the **Abs()** function. This function will return the absolute value of a number. Taking the absolute value of a number will remove any negative sign and leave a positive number. So, for example, the absolute value of the number 2 is 2, and the absolute value of -2 is also 2.

The **Abs()** function accepts a numeric input and produces a numeric output:

```
result = Abs(numberValue)
```

This function takes only one parameter: **numberValue**. The **Abs()** function will then return the absolute value of this parameter and you can assign that answer to some other variable.

Another useful math function is the square root function: **Sqr()**. The **Sqr()** function will return the square root of a number. The **Sqr()** function looks like this:

```
result = Sqr(numberValue)
```

This function also only takes one parameter: the number for which you want the square root. The **Sqr()** function will then return the square root value of this number. The parameter must be greater than zero!

Lesson Three: Using Math in Programs

In this lesson, we will create a simple calculator program. Open up the Visual Basic IDE and create a new project called "Calculator". Use the property sheet to change the **(Name)** of the form to "CalculatorForm" and the **Text** of the form to "My Calculator".

Next, we will add two new controls to our form. These controls are called "NumericUpDown" controls, and are specially made to handle number-only input. An example "NumericUpDown" control is shown to the right:

This control actually contains 2 elements: a textbox (the white box with the number "4"), and a "spinner" control, which will allow a user to increase or decrease the number by one just by clicking on the arrows. This means that a user can either enter their number into the box, or use the arrows to "spin" the control to the correct number. The best thing about using this control is that a user is only allowed to use a number in the box. This keeps users from accidentally entering text when you expect them to enter a number!

To retrieve a user's value from these controls in a program, we can just access the **Value** property of the control, just like we would use the **Text** property of a textbox. Here is an example:

```
Dim theUsersNumber As Integer
theUsersNumber = myNumericUpDown.Value
```

The **Value** property is actual a **Decimal** data type, so you can enter fractional numbers if needed!

Now, back to our new program! On the form, add the following controls:
- Two "NumericUpDown" buttons:
    - One with the **(Name)** "FirstNumber"
    - One with the **(Name)** "SecondNumber".
- A Textbox control with the **(Name)** "ResultTextbox".
- An Add button with the **(Name)** of "AddButton" and text of "Add".
- A Subtract button with the **(Name)** of "SubtractButton" and text of "Subtract".

You should end up with a form that looks like this:

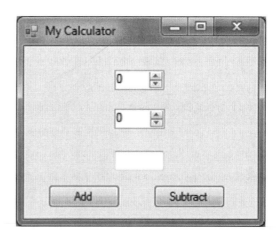

Now we will add some code to our buttons. We will be expecting the user to change the numbers in the NumericUpDown controls by either typing in some digits, or using the spinner to select their number.

Double-click on the "Add" button to bring up the code window for the "Add" button's click function.

We should have two values from the user, one in the **FirstNumber** control and one in the **SecondNumber** control. So just add them together, convert the result to a string, and place the string into our **ResultTextbox** control.

```
ResultTextbox.Text = Str(FirstNumber.Value + SecondNumber.Value)
```

Our final code looks something like this:

```
Private Sub AddButton_Click(ByVal sender As System.Object, _
                        ByVal e As System.EventArgs) _
                        Handles AddButton.Click
        ResultTextbox.Text = Str(FirstNumber.Value + SecondNumber.Value)
End Sub
```

Now we will add the same code to our "Subtract" button, changing the line that computes the value of our **ResultTextbox** from addition to subtraction. Double-click on the "Subtract" button and bring up the code window for the "Subtract" button even handler. As you can guess the "Subtract" code is very similar to the "Add" button. Go ahead and complete this function in your program now:

```
Private Sub SubtractButton_Click(ByVal sender As System.Object, _
                        ByVal e As System.EventArgs) _
                        Handles SubtractButton.Click


        ResultTextbox.Text = Str(FirstNumber.Value - SecondNumber.Value)
End Sub
```

Again, the only thing that is different is that here we are setting the **ResultTextbox** equal to the difference of our two numbers Now go ahead and try the program! Do both the addition and subtraction buttons work correctly?

Make sure you remember to save your project when you close the application. To do this, click on "File" and "Close Project". Name your project "Calculator", make sure you are saving in your "C:\KidCoder\Windows Programming\My Projects" directory, and name your solution "Calculator".

Chapter Review

- The **Str**() function will convert a number to a string

- The **Val**() function will convert a string to a number.

- Use the **IsNumeric**() function to see if a string can be converted to a number.

- Math operations (add, subtract, multiply and divide) are done with the math operators: +, -, * and /.

- You should never attempt to divide any number by 0, since this will cause a program error.

- There are many helper math functions that perform common tasks.

- The **Abs**() function will return the absolute value of a number.

- The **Sqr**() function will return the square root of a number.

Your Turn: Grade Calculator

In this activity, you will write a new program similar to the Calculator program that we just created. This new program will allow a user to enter 5 different grades and then will calculate the average score for these grades. To find an average, you need to add up your values and then divide by the number of values. In our case, we will add the 5 grades together and then divide by 5.

Open up the Visual Basic IDE and create a new project called "Grade Calculator". Use the property sheet to change the **(Name)** of the form to "GradeForm" and the **Text** of the form to "Grade Calculator".

On your form, you will need to add the following controls:

- Five "NumericUpDown" buttons. The **(Name)** of these controls should be: "FirstGrade", "SecondGrade", "ThirdGrade", "FourthGrade", and "FifthGrade".
- A Textbox control with the **(Name)** "AverageTextbox".
- A label control which describes the AverageTextbox with something like: "Grade Average:"
- A button with the **(Name)** "AverageButton". Change the button **Text** to: "Average the Grades!"

Your form should now look something like this:

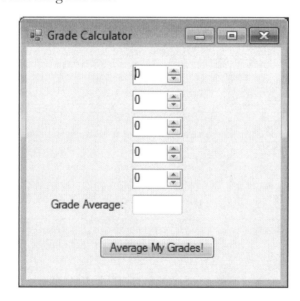

Then you will need to do the following:

- Double-click the **AverageButton** button to add code to the "click" event.
- Create a **Double** variable called **totalGrades** to hold the total sum of all of the grade values.
- Set the value of **totalGrades** equal to the sum of all of the grade values.
- Set the **ResultTextbox.Text** property equal to the value of **totalGrades** divided by 5.

Now run your program and see if your grade average is calculated correctly when you hit the button! For example, the average of the inputs 90, 100, 100, 80, and 85 is equal to 91.

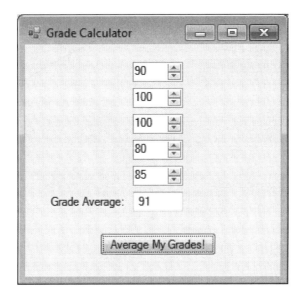

Chapter Eight: Working with Strings

We have already used simple strings in our programs. Now we are going to look at characters and strings in more detail.

Lesson One: Initializing Chars and Strings

This lesson will describe some of the ways to declare character and string data types. We will also discuss the computer memory used by the two data types.

Visual Basic Char

The **Char** data type is used to hold a single character in memory. This is especially useful for storing things like a middle initial in a name, a "Y" (yes) or "N" (no) answer to a question or any single special character. If you know that you will be only storing one character, use this data type since it takes less computer memory than a **String**.

The format for declaring a **Char** variable looks like this:

```
Dim variableName As Char
```

So, if we wanted to use a **Char** for storing a person's middle initial, we could declare the following:

```
Dim middleInitial As Char
```

We can assign a single character value to the **Char** variable using a simple assignment statement:

```
middleInitial = "K"
```

We can also test a **Char** variable using logical expressions and conditional operators like this:

```
If (middleInitial = "R") Then
     ' do something here
End If
```

Visual Basic Strings

A group of characters put together is commonly called a "string". A string can be a word ("Hello") or a sentence ("This is my string.") or even a group of sentences. In Visual Basic, the data type that can handle any text is, of course, called a **String**.

The format for declaring a **String** variable looks like this:

```
Dim variableName As String
```

Initializing Strings

In order to use a string, you will need to assign it a value. This is called *initializing* your string (since you are putting an initial value into it). A **String** variable that has been created or declared, but not initialized, has a value of **Nothing** (also commonly called "null"). **Nothing** is a special value; and is not equal to an empty or a zero-length string. Any variable that equals **Nothing** has no data at all in it...not even a blank string! If you attempt to use a **String** value containing **Nothing** your program may crash!

Strings are initialized by assigning a group of characters to a string variable.

```
myString = "Hello"
```

If you are setting your **String** to a specific text value, that value must be enclosed in quotes. If you are setting your **String** to the value of another variable, you do not need to use quotes. For example, if both **myString** and **yourString** were **String** variables, you can assign the contents of **yourString** to **myString** using an assignment statement like this:

```
myString = yourString
```

You can declare and initialize your **String** at the same time. For example:

```
Dim myString As String = "Hello"
```

The above example creates a variable called **myString** and assigns the value "Hello" to it in one step!

Lesson Two: String Operators and Functions

Sometimes you will need to compare or concatenate (glue together) two strings. Visual Basic defines some simple operators to make these tasks easy to code and read. Visual Basic also defines a number of useful functions that let you determine the length of strings and change the case of strings.

String Comparison

String comparison operators allow you to compare the contents of two strings.

The first comparison operator is the "equal to" operator "=". The "=" character will form a logical expression that returns true if two strings are exactly the same. This might be useful if you were checking a user's password to see if it matches the password in the computer's memory. Here is an example of using the "equal to" operator to form a logical expression that is then tested by an **If()** statement:

```
If (string1 = string2) Then
     ' do something here
End if
```

It is important to remember that the expression (**string1 = string2**) will only be true if the two strings are EXACTLY alike. The letters and their cases must be identical. The string "Hello" is not equal to the string "hello" because the case of the first letter "h" is different.

You may also want to perform a check to see if two strings are not equal to one another. This is done with the "not equal" operator "<>". You use this operator exactly like the "equal to" operator except the logical expression will return true if the strings are different. For example:

```
If (string1 <> string2) Then
     ' do something here
End if
```

Again, remember that this comparison is case-sensitive.

String Concatenation

String *concatenation* operators will join (glue together) two or more strings together to make one large string. There are two concatenation operators: "+" and "&". Both of these operators will join a string and have an almost identical syntax. The following two statements do the same thing:

```
myString = "This " + "is " + "my " + "string"
myString = "This " & "is " & "my " & "string"
```

Both of these statements will assign "This is my string" to the variable **myString**. Notice that we used spaces within the quotes after each word when we built our string. The "&" and "+" operators will not add spaces in between the words; you have to do that yourself!

When concatenating strings it is important to remember to add spaces between your strings when needed. This can make the difference between a string "like this" and a string "likethis". If you don't add spaces, your words will run together!

The plus sign (+) is typically used to add two numbers together, though it will also work to concatenate strings. The "&" operator is used only for string concatenation, and it will automatically convert the parameters on either side to string before joining them. In order to avoid confusion, it is usually best to just use the "&" operator when joining strings.

vbNewLine

In addition to joining strings of text, you can add some formatting to your strings with the help of a built-in character called **vbNewLine**. This special character can be added to a string at a point where you want the next part to start on a new line. For example, if you were to display a string in a message box like this:

```
MsgBox("My address is: 129 Peachtree St Atlanta GA 30001")
```

You would see the following message box:

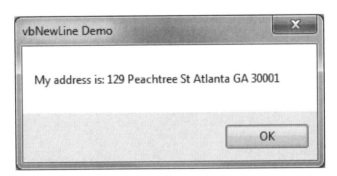

This is readable, but not exactly the way we are used to looking at an address. Instead, we can improve the look of this message by using a **vbNewLine** character:

```
MsgBox("My address is:" & vbNewLine & _
       "129 Peachtree St" & vbNewLine & _
       "Atlanta GA 30001")
```

Now the message box will show the address broken across three lines as shown to the right.

The **vbNewLine** character is a great help in formatting longer strings into more readable blocks of text.

Changing Cases

Visual Basic has two functions that will change the case of the letters in a string: **UCase()** and **LCase()**.

The **UCase()** function changes all of the letters in a string to upper-case. You use the function like this:

```
Dim resultString As String = UCase(myString)
```

The input parameter can be a string variable (e.g. **myString**) or a hard-coded string like "my string". Either way the function output will be a string containing all upper-case letters. So, for example, **UCase**("look out!") would return "LOOK OUT!".

The **LCase()** function changes all of the letters in a string to lower-case. You use the function like this:

```
Dim resultString As String = LCase(myString)
```

The function output will be a string containing all lower-case letters. As you probably expect, **LCase**("WOW") returns "wow".

Length of Strings

Sometimes it is useful to know the *string length*, or how many characters a string contains. The **Len()** function will tell you the length of an input string. The **Len()** function is used like this:

```
Dim resultInteger As Integer = Len(myString)
```

This function takes a string as input and returns the number of characters in the string. In the above example, if your **myString** variable contained the text "This is a string", the **Len()** function would return a length of 16 (which includes letters and spaces).

This function is especially useful if you want to validate user text input. For example, if you ask the user to input a zip code, you know the text should have exactly 5 characters...no more, and no less. The **Len()** function will help you to determine if the user entered the right number of digits.

Reversing Strings

Reversing a string means you swap the order of all the characters so the resulting string is backwards when compared to the input string. For instance, the reverse of "abc" is "cba" and the reverse of "the quick brown fox" is "xof nworb kciuq eht". The **StrReverse()** function which will perform this task.

```
Dim resultString As String = StrReverse(myString)
```

This function takes the input string (a string variable or static text) and returns the reverse string as output.

Selecting Parts of a String

In addition to changing the content of a string, there are a few functions which can be used to select only a part of a string.

We can copy certain parts of a string by using the **Strings.Left()** and **Strings.Right()** functions. Unlike the other string functions, you must call these by using "Strings." on the front! This is because your Form also has **Left** and **Right** properties, and we need to tell Visual Basic that we're using the functions dealing with strings instead!

The **Strings.Left()** function is used to pull a number of characters from the left (beginning) of the string. Here's an example using the **Strings.Left()** function:

```
Dim firstString As String = "Jack Sprat"
Dim newString As String = Strings.Left(firstString, 4)
```

When you run this code, you would see the value "Jack" placed into the **newString** variable.

You can do something similar with the **Strings.Right()** function. This function will copy characters from the right side (end) of a string. Here's another example using the **Right()** function:

```
Dim firstString As String = "Jack Sprat"
Dim newString As String = Strings.Right(firstString, 5)
```

After this code is run, the value of the **newString** variable would be "Sprat".

 Always use the prefix "Strings." when using the Left() and Right() string functions. This is because your Form also has a Left and Right property. The "String." prefix tells Visual Basic that we want to use the String Left() or Right() function, not the Form properties!

Lesson Three: Using Strings in a Program

In this lesson you will create a new project to practice the string functions that we have learned.

Open the Visual Basic IDE and create a new project called "Strings". Click on the Form and change the **(Name)** to "StringForm" and the **Text** to "Working With Strings".

Next create three buttons at the bottom of the form:

- The first button's **(Name)** should be "UpperButton" and its **Text** should be "Upper Case".
- The second button's **(Name)** should be "LowerButton" and its **Text** should be "Lower Case".
- The third button's **(Name)** should be "CompareButton" and its **Text** should be "Compare".

Your form so far looks something like this:

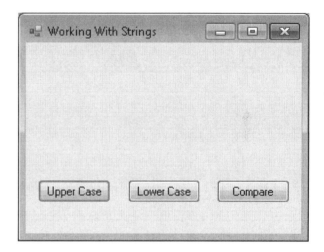

Now add two textboxes that our users can use to enter two strings of text. We will use the default **(Name)** and **Text** properties for these controls.

We will also add two labels, one above each textbox, which will tell our user what information to enter. There is no need to change the **(Name)** of each label, but set the **Text** values to the following:

- The first label should say: "Enter your first string:"
- The second label should say: "Enter your second string:"

Your form should now look like this:

We are ready to enter the code for our buttons! Double-click on the "Upper Case" button to bring up the code window for the button handler function. We will use this button to change the contents of the textboxes to upper case letters. To do this, add the following code:

```
TextBox1.Text = UCase(TextBox1.Text)
TextBox2.Text = UCase(TextBox2.Text)
```

Since we didn't change the name of the two textboxes, the default names are **Textbox1** and **Textbox2**. Notice that we use the **.Text** property of the text box as input to the **UCase()** function. We assign the output of the function right back into the **.Text** property in order to update the text box control!

Now we will add some code to the "Lower Case" button. Double-click on the button to bring up the code window for the button handler function. Add the following code:

```
TextBox1.Text = LCase(TextBox1.Text)
TextBox2.Text = LCase(TextBox2.Text)
```

This button will now do the exact opposite of the "Upper Case" button; it will set the contents of the textboxes to all lower case letters.

Finally, let's make the "Compare" button work! Double-click on this button to create the event handler function. This button will tell the user whether or not the two strings are the same. Add the following code:

```
If (TextBox1.Text = TextBox2.Text) Then
        MsgBox("The strings are the same")
Else
        MsgBox("The strings are not the same")
End If
```

Here we use an **If()** statement to decide which **MsgBox()** to show to the user. If the contents of the two textboxes are the same, we pop-up the message: "The strings are the same". If the contents are not the same, we pop-up the message: "The strings are not the same".

Now run your program and test the buttons!

You may wish to compare strings and ignore any differences in upper or lower case letters. Perhaps you asked the user to type in "yes" or "no" to a question, and wanted to identify "Yes", "yes", "YES", or even "yEs" as a valid "yes" response. To do this you can use the **LCase**() or **UCase**() functions to ensure both strings are entirely upper or lower case before performing the equals check!

Here's an example that will evaluate to **True** if the string value converted to lower case equals "yes":

```
If (LCase(stringValue) = "yes") Then
      ' do something here
End If
```

 Make sure you remember to save your project when you close the application. To do this, click on "File" and "Close Project". Name your project "Strings", make sure you are saving in your "C:\KidCoder\Windows Programming\My Projects" directory, and name your solution "Strings".

 **Chapter Review**

- The **Char** data type is used to hold a single character or letter. The **String** data type is used to hold one or more characters or letters.

- Strings can be initialized with no value (**Nothing**) or some specified text.

- There are many built-in functions that let you evaluate or change the contents of a string.

- You can join together two strings using the "+" or "&" operators, though "&" is most commonly used for strings.

- You can use the **UCase**() and **LCase**() functions to convert a string to all upper or lower case letters.

- You can use the **Len**() function to determine the number of characters in a string.

- You can use the **StrReverse**() function to rearrange the string contents from back to front.

- You can use the **Strings.Left**() and **Strings.Right**() functions to get parts of the string from the left or right sides.

Your Turn: Pig Latin Translator

In this activity, we will be creating a new program which will translate a single word into Pig Latin. Translating words into "Pig Latin" is easy! If the word starts with a vowel, you just add the letters "-way" to the end of the word. If the word starts with a consonant, you take the first letter and place it at the end of the word, then add the letters "-ay" to the end of the word.

For example: the word "hello" is translated "elloh-ay" in Pig Latin. The word "okay" is translated as "okay-way". Notice that there is a dash between the original word and the letters "way" or "ay". This is just a way of making the Pig Latin translation stand out in a word.

Open up the Visual Basic IDE and create a new project called "Pig Latin Translator". Click on the Form and change the **(Name)** to "PigLatinForm" and the **Text** to "Pig Latin Translator".

Now you will need to do the following:

- Add two textbox controls: one with a **(Name)** of "OriginalText" and one with a **(Name)** of "TranslatedText"
- Add two label controls for the textboxes: one with the text: "Enter a word:" and the second with the text: "Your word in Pig Latin:"
- Add a button control with the **(Name)** "TranslateButton" and the text: "Translate!"

At this point, your form should look something like this:

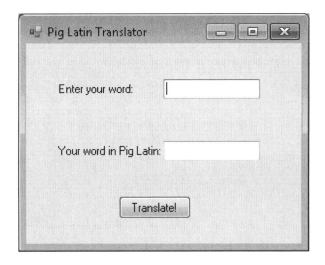

Then you will need to do the following:

- Double-click the "Translate!" button to add code to the "click" event.
- Within your translate click event function, declare these variables:
    - A **String** variable named **stringInput** to hold the text from in the first textbox.
    - A **String** variable named **resultString** to hold the Pig Latin translation
    - A **Char** variable named **firstCharacter** to hold the first character of the user's word
    - An **Integer** variable called **stringLength** to hold the length of the user's word
- Set the **stringInput** variable equal to the text in the **OriginalText** textbox. Change the letters to lower case when assigning to the **stringInput** variable.
- Set the **stringLength** variable equal to the length of the **stringInput** text.
- Set the **firstCharacter** variable equal to the first character in **stringInput**. (Hint: Use the **Strings.Left**() method!)
- Use an **If** statement to decide if the **firstCharacter** value is a vowel ("a", "e", "i", "o", or "u"). Don't forget you can use the **Or** operator to join together several logical expressions!
    - If the **firstCharacter** is a vowel, set the **resultString** value to the value in **stringInput** and then add the letters "-way" to the end.
    - If the **firstCharacter** is not a vowel, set the **resultString** value to the value in **stringInput** (minus the first letter), add the "-" character, the **firstCharacter** value and then the letters "ay"
- Finally, set the **TranslatedText.Text** to the value in **resultString** so the answer will appear in the form!

Run your program and check your Pig Latin conversion! Try both "hello" and "okay" as we described above, and also use your own words.

Chapter Nine: Using the Debugger

Normally, when you run a program, it runs directly on top of the operating system. You can also run a special program called a *debugger* which sits between your program and the operating system. The debugger can help you find bugs (errors) in your program!

Lesson One: Debugger Concepts

A debugger will let you walk step-by-step through each line in your program and observe your program as it runs. This is an extremely powerful tool. While you are watching the running program, you can make sure the program is working as you expect. This includes making sure the statements are executing in the correct order and even watching the contents of your variables to make sure the data is being stored correctly.

Most importantly, when an error occurs, you can figure out exactly which line caused the error!

Program States

While you are running your program in the debugger, your program will be in one of two states: *running* or *in-break*.

When your program is in the running state, it is executing normally. The program starts at the beginning and responds to events as normal. This isn't the most useful state for debugging. When you are in this state the program is moving far too fast to watch individual statements or look at the data.

When your program is in-break, it is paused or suspended. The debugger knows the complete state of the program, including what statement is about to be run and what data is contained in all variables. While in-break, most debuggers will highlight the program statement that is *about* to be run. The statement above has already been run and the one that is highlighted will be run next. You can see in the example below that the statement with the **UCase()** function call is currently highlighted, meaning that statement is the next one that will be executed.

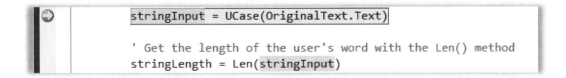

```
stringInput = UCase(OriginalText.Text)

' Get the length of the user's word with the Len() method
stringLength = Len(stringInput)
```

We'll have more about the in-break state in the next lesson!

 The most useful state for debugging is in the "in-break" state. In this state your program is paused or frozen. While in-break you can look at the values in your variables and watch your program execute line-by-line.

Debugging Commands

Most debuggers, including the one that comes with Visual Basic, will support the same general set of commands. While in-break you can run one of the debugging commands described below to make your program continue with the next statement(s).

Run or Continue

If your program is not running, this command will start running your program in the debugger. If you are already debugging the program and are in-break, this command will put the program back into the running state. The program will run until it reaches the end of the program or until a breakpoint is reached (we'll talk about breakpoints below).

Step Over

This command will execute the current statement and then stop again at the next statement. This allows you to examine the results of the statement that was just executed. Did your variables get updated as expected? Did your program flow statements such as **If()** work correctly? Walking through a program in the debugger is often referred to as "stepping through" a program.

Stop

The Stop command will completely end your program; no more statements will be executed. You can then edit or modify your code, build, and run it again.

Breakpoints

It would not take too long to "step through" most of the small programs you have seen so far, starting at the beginning and then stepping through each line of code until the end. For larger programs, however, it can take a long time to step through many lines of code. Often you want the program to run normally until it reaches a certain section of code, or until some event happens. This is where *breakpoints* come into play!

You can set a breakpoint on any of the statements in your code. When the debugger reaches a statement with a breakpoint it will halt the program in-break mode. When the program is in-break, you can view the data in your variables at that exact point in the program. For GUI programs like we are creating in Visual Basic, most of your code belongs to event handler functions. You can put a breakpoint inside these functions so your program will enter break mode when you click on a specific button.

You can set as many breakpoints in your program as you like. Each of the above commands (Continue, Step Over, etc...) will automatically stop and put the program in break mode whenever a breakpoint is hit, no matter how far the program would have otherwise run according to the command.

Lesson Two: Stepping Through a Program in the Debugger

In this lesson we will create a simple program that contains one (or more) bugs. We will use this program to practice looking at variable contents, setting breakpoints and stepping through our program.

Open the Visual Basic IDE and create a new project called "Guess My Number". Change the Form's **(Name)** to "GuessForm" and its **Text** to "Guess My Number". Then add a textbox with the **(Name)** of "NumberTextbox" and a label with the **Text** of "Enter your number:". Finally, add a button named "GuessButton" and give it a **Text** value of "Make a Guess". Your final form is shown on the right.

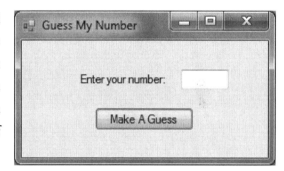

Now we can add some code to our "Make A Guess" button. Double-click the button to bring up the code window and add the following code to the button's click function:

```
Dim myNumber As Integer = 5

Dim theirNumber As Integer = NumberTextBox.Text

If (theirNumber = myNumber) Then
    MsgBox("You guessed it!")

ElseIf (theirNumber > myNumber) Then
    MsgBox("Try something higher!")

ElseIf (theirNumber < myNumber) Then
    MsgBox("Try something lower!")

End If
```

This is a really simple program that just asks the user to guess the number that the program has stored in the **myNumber** variable. In our case, the value of this variable is "5". If the user guesses a number that is too low, a **MsgBox** should tell the user to try something higher. If the user guesses a number that is too high, a **MsgBox** should tell the user to try something lower. If they guess correctly, a **MsgBox** will tell them the good news.

Note: Make sure you add the code EXACTLY as you see it above. When you're done, the program will compile and run – but it still contains some problems!

Starting In the Debugger

In order to start the debugger, we will just hit the same button that we have been using to run our programs: the ▶ button. Go ahead and press that button now to start the program. You should see your form appear on the screen. Enter the number "3" and press the "Make a Guess" button. You should see the following message box:

Hmmm… Something is not quite right! We know that the secret number is "5". We guessed the number "3". Shouldn't the program have told us to guess higher? Let's try the number "7":

Well that's not right either! Our number is already higher than the secret number!

Setting Breakpoints

In order to debug our program, we need to set some breakpoints. This will let us stop the program and walk through some code as it runs. Open the code window for the "Guess My Number" project and set your cursor on the first line of the "**If**" statement. To set the breakpoint, you can press the F9 key, or click on Debug menu item and choose "Toggle Breakpoint", or you can right-click on the line of code and choose "Breakpoint" and then "Insert Breakpoint". All of these methods will result in a breakpoint being set at the selected line. Once you have set a breakpoint, your window should look like this:

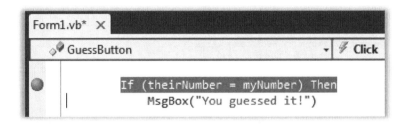

Now when we run the program, the debugger will stop when we reach this line of code. Go ahead and run your program, enter the number "3" again and then click on the "Make a Guess" button. The program will pause and pop-up the code window when you reach the breakpoint.

Once the program is in-break, you will see a yellow arrow in the red breakpoint circle and the current line of code will be highlighted in yellow. This line has not yet been executed!

Looking at Variable Contents

Now that we are in-break on our "**If**" statement, let's see what values we have in our variables. Move your mouse cursor until it is over **theirNumber**. You will see something like this:

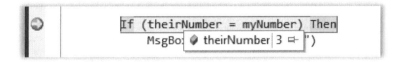

Notice the pop-up box that says: "theirNumber 3". The debugger will show you the value of a variable when you hold the mouse cursor over it. You can hold the mouse pointer over the **myNumber** variable and see what is in that variable as well.

Another way to view the contents of variables while in-break is to add the variable to the "watch" window. This will make the variable appear at the bottom of the code window while the program is in-break mode. To do this, right-click on the variable name (in our case: **theirNumber**) and choose "Add Watch". You will see the following window at the bottom of the code window:

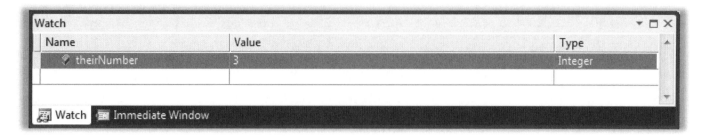

Now every time you execute a statement in-break mode, the Watch window will show you the new value of all variables you are watching!

Stepping Through the Program

Now we will take another step into our program by executing the line that we have been looking at. To do this, click on the Debug menu and then click on "Step Over" or just hit the Shift+F8 keys. This will execute the current line and move to the next line of code. You should now see the next **If** statement highlighted. This statement has not yet been executed, but it will be when we "Step Over" again. We should see the code beneath this **If** statement execute next. Use the "Step Over" command now and see what happens!

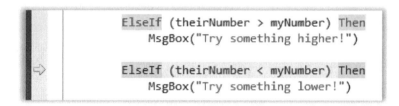

Uh-oh! Instead of highlighting the "**MsgBox**("Try something higher!") line of code, the program thinks the next line should be the next **If** statement. This means that it evaluated the previous **If** statement as **False**. Let's take a closer look at the previous **If** statement:

```
ElseIf(theirNumber > myNumber) Then
```

Can you see the problem with this statement? We have accidentally reversed our greater than and less than signs! Instead of checking to see if **theirNumber** is less than **myNumber**, we are checking to see if **theirNumber** is greater than **myNumber**. If you look at the next **If** statement, you can see that we have reversed that sign as well.

Go ahead and change the signs right now. Then press the ▶ button. This should display the program form again. Enter the number set to "3" and press the "Make a Guess" button again. Your program will break at the first **If** statement. Use the "Step Over" button to walk through the program and watch the statements execute. This time, you should see the line "**MsgBox**("Try something higher!") run as expected.

Great job! You have fixed your program's bug by using the Visual Basic Debugger!

Lesson Three: Runtime Exceptions

In some computer programming languages an unexpected error will cause the whole program to crash in weird ways. In the Visual Basic language, an unexpected error will cause (or "throw") an *exception*. Exceptions are errors that cause a program to change its normal program flow. This means that the code statements that occur after the problem statement will not be executed. Instead, the program will show a warning message on the screen. This message will appear whether you are running in the debugger or running in normal execution mode, and will describe the nature of the error. You will then have a choice of closing the program, attempting to continue to program or getting more detailed information.

One common exception that occurs in a program is called a "divide by zero" exception. This problem happens when a programmer attempts to divide any number by the number zero. If you know your division rules, you know that you cannot divide a number by zero! A computer cannot divide by zero either!

Exceptions in the Debugger

Let's create a quick program which contains an error that will throw an exception. Open the Visual Basic IDE and create a new project called "Exception Error". Create a single button on the form (pick your own name and text) and add the following code to the "Click" event for the button:

```
Dim bottom As Integer = 0
Dim top As Integer = 1

' the next line raises a divide-by-zero exception
Dim result As Integer
result = top / bottom
```

Now if you start the program and push the button, the program will stop and automatically throw you into the Visual Basic Debugger with a message like this:

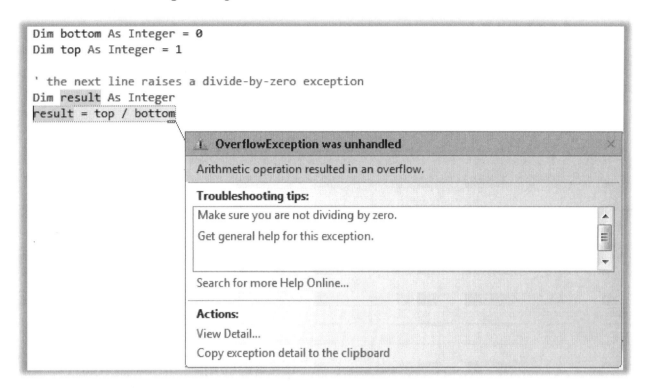

This is very handy since the IDE has pointed us to the exact line that caused the problem and has given us some great advice in the "Troubleshooting Tips" section. The tips tell us that we need to make sure we are not "dividing by zero". At this point, since we are in debugging mode, you can hold your mouse over the "bottom" variable and check to see if it is equal to zero:

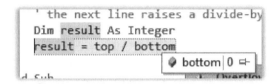

Sure enough! Our program is trying to divide a number by zero. Of course, we already knew that, but you can see how this is an invaluable tool when solving errors in your programs!

Exceptions at Runtime

The last example showed what happens when we get an exception while running in the Visual Basic debugger. But what happens if someone installs our program on their computer and tries to run the program?. In the case of our divide-by-zero program, Visual Basic will throw an exception that looks something like this:

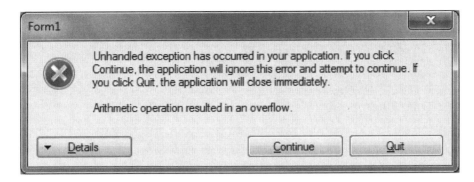

At this point, your program has basically stopped working. We cannot switch to the Visual Basic Debugger, since we are not running this out of the Visual Basic IDE. Instead, we need to use the information in this message to figure out what went wrong. The text of the message gives us some idea of the source of the error: "Arithmetic operation resulted in an overflow". In order to find out more information about this error, we can click on the "Details" button.

The "Details" button will most likely list the specific location of the error. Now you know exactly where your program went wrong!

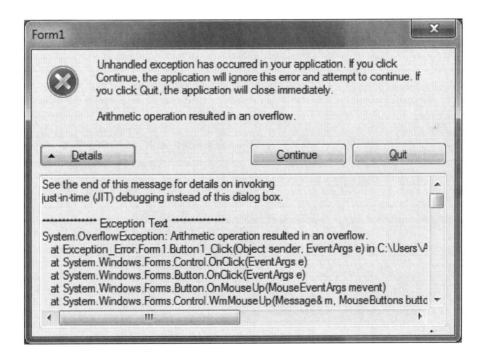

In the case of our divide-by-zero program, the exception details area shows that the error occurred when "Form1.Button1" was clicked. Now we can go back to our program and take a look at that code.

In addition to the "Details" button, you have a choice of "Continue" and "Quit". If you click on the "Continue" button, your program will attempt to continue. Typically a program will not run very well after an exception is thrown, but you can always try!

If you click on the "Quit" button, the program will end immediately. This is a much easier and cleaner way to end a misbehaving program! You can then either debug the program or try to run it again.

 ## Chapter Review

- A debugger is a piece of software that sits between the program and the operating system. This software allows a programmer to "step through" their program line-by-line.

- A program can be in two states while executing under the debugger: running and in-break.

- The in-break state is much more useful for debugging than the "running" state.

- A debugger supports several useful commands: Run, Step Over, and Continue.

- A breakpoint is where you want the debugger to put the program in-break mode so that you can look at the variables and step through the code.

- You can look at variable contents by holding the mouse cursor over the variable name, or by adding the variable to the "watch" window.

- Serious program errors may result in an exception being thrown.

- When running in the debugger, an exception message will tell you exactly which line caused the error.

Your Turn: Guess My Letter?

In this activity you will continue to use the "Guess My Number" created during this chapter.

Open the "Guess My Number" project again. To do this, run the Visual Basic IDE and click on "File" and "Open Project". Your project should have been saved in "C:\KidCoder\Windows Programming\My Projects\Guess My Number" and the filename should be "Guess My Number.sln". Select this file to open the project. If you do not see your project's screen and code, just use the Solution Explorer icons to display those screens.

For this activity, you will fix the second hidden bug in this program. To do this, run the program and enter a *letter* such as "A" instead of a number in the textbox. Press the "Make a Guess" button and watch your program explode! Now you will need to find and fix this bug!

Find the line of code that is causing the error and fix this line of code so that this error does not appear again. Hint: Remember our discussion about input validation in Chapter Six!

Chapter Ten: Loops in Programs

Sometimes you will want your program to execute the same group of statements more than one time. Let's take for example a program that prints out the names and test scores for 10 students. This program would need a series of statements that printed the students' first name, last name and test score. We could write a set of these statements for each student, but that would mean a lot of repeated code. Instead what we will do is *loop through* one set of statements 10 times. This is called *program loop control*.

In this chapter you will learn about three different kinds of loops.

Lesson One: For Loops

One common loop is a *"For loop"*. This type of loop will execute a set of statements a fixed number of times. This would be the perfect loop technique for the student example above if we knew ahead of time exactly how many students are in the group.

For Loop Syntax

All **For** loops are based on an *index*, which is a numeric variable (typically an **Integer**). The index starts at some number and is then increased or decreased each time through the loop until the ending number is reached.

The format of a **For** loop looks like this:

```
For myIndex = numberToStartAt To numberToEndAt (Step numberToCountBy)
        ' execute these statements
Next
```

Let's look at the syntax line-by-line:

```
For myIndex = numberToStartAt To numberToEndAt (Step numberToCountBy)
```

The first word in this line is just the **For** keyword, which tells the program that we will be starting a **For** loop. After the **For** keyword is an assignment statement ("**myIndex** = **numberToStartAt**" in this example) that sets our index variable equal to some starting number, usually 1 or 0. The index variable will be increased or decreased each time we execute our loop. You must declare the index variable before the beginning of the **For** loop.

The next element in this line is the **To** keyword. Following **To** is the **numberToEndAt** which tells the **For** loop how large or small the index variable can get before the looping stops.

The final item on the first line is the keyword **Step** and then the **numberToCountBy**. The **numberToCountBy** is the number that you want to add to the index after every loop is completed. Most of the time you will just want to add 1 to your index every time, but you could add 2 or 3 or any other integer. The default step is 1, so you don't have to use the **Step** keyword if 1 is what you want to add each time through the loop.

The next line in our example is actually a placeholder for any number of statements:

```
' execute these statements
```

This is where we want to put the code that will be executed each time the loop runs. You can have one or any number of statements that will execute each time through the loop. Don't forget you can use the index variable itself within the loop, but don't change it! Let the **For** loop itself change the index variable each time through.

The final line, **Next**, tells our program that we have reached the end of the loop and it's time to start at the top of the loop again. When the **Next** statement is reached the index variable will be changed by the amount you specified by the **Step** value in the **For** loop. If the index variable is less than or equal to the number we want to end at, program flow will continue at the top of the loop body again. If the index variable is greater than the number we want to end at, then the program will exit the loop and continue executing the statements after the **Next** keyword.

Exit Keyword

There may be times when you want to exit a **For** loop before the loop has been normally completed. To do this, you can use the **Exit For** keywords, like this:

```
For i = 1 To 5
    MsgBox(i)
    Exit For    ' break out of the For loop right now
Next
MsgBox("after for")
```

In this example you will only see one **MsgBox** pop-up showing the value 1, then the loop will end and you will see the "after for" message displayed next. You can also use this same "Exit" concept on the **While** and **Do-While** loops we describe in the next lesson! Just use the **Exit While** or Exit **Do** keywords instead.

Example For Loop

This simple **For** loop will execute 5 times and will print out the current value of the index variable: "**i**".

```
Dim i As Integer
For i = 0 To 4 Step 1
     MsgBox("We are now on loop number: " & i)
Next
```

This loop will show the following messages, one at a time:

```
We are now on loop number: 0
We are now on loop number: 1
We are now on loop number: 2
We are now on loop number: 3
We are now on loop number: 4
```

Notice that the loop body will execute when "**i = 4**" because that is equal to the number at which we want to stop. When the counter (the variable "**i**") is greater than the ending number, the loop will end.

Lesson Two: While Loops and Do-While Loops

The second type of program loop is called a *"while loop"*. This type of loop is used to execute a set of statements *while* a condition is true. You may not know in advance how many times the loop will execute, but you know when the loop should continue and when it should stop. For instance, you may want to continue obtaining user input until the user sends some special signal that they are done. So you would loop *while* the user input is *not equal* to that special signal.

While Loops

A **While** loop is based on a logical expression that evaluates to either **True** or **False**. As long as this expression evaluates to **True**, the loop will continue to execute. The **While** loop syntax looks like this:

```
While (condition)
     ' execute these statements
End While
```

Let's look at this syntax line by line.

The first line is: "**While** (condition)". **While** is just a keyword that tells the program that we will be using a **While** loop. The (condition) is a logical expression that will decide whether or not to continue looping.

Continuing our student example from the last lesson, our logical expression could be something like: "**studentNumber < 5**".

The second line represents the set of statements that we want to execute every time the loop is run. The last line contains the keywords **End While**, which marks the end of our **While** loop.

The most important difference between a **For** loop and a **While** loop is that the **While** loop does not have an index variable. The condition is a logical expression that may contain any valid test such as "**userInput <> "q"** " or "**studentNumber < 5**". It is possible that the statements within the **While** loop *never* execute if the condition evaluates to **False** when the program first reaches the loop!

It is very important that the condition expression be updated by the statements within the **While** loop! There must be some way for the expression to eventually become **False**; otherwise the program will get stuck in the loop forever. This condition is called an "infinite loop".

For instance, let's say we want to run a loop 10 times and our counter variable is called "**loopCounter**". We know that our logical expression is "**loopCounter < 10**". We will need to increase the value of "**loopCounter**" ourselves each time through the loop. The **While** statement will NOT do it for you. If you never increase this variable, the logical expression will never be **False**, and your **While** loop will execute forever.

If we were to re-write our example 5-step **For** loop as a **While** loop, it would look like this:

```
Dim loopCounter As Integer = 0
While loopCounter < 5
    MsgBox("We are now at loop number: " & loopCounter )
    loopCounter = loopCounter + 1
End While
```

Do-While Loops

The last type of loop that we will discuss is called the "*Do-While loop*". The **Do-While** loop is nearly the same as the **While** loop since it is based on a logical expression that evaluates to either **True** or **False**. As long as this condition is **True**, the loop will continue to execute. The difference is that the expression is tested at the bottom of the loop instead of the top! A bottom-tested **Do-While** loop will test the loop condition after the loop is executed at least one time. A top-tested **While** loop may never execute because its loop condition is tested before the loop runs the first time. A bottom-tested loop will always execute at least once, since its loop condition is not tested until the bottom of the loop!

It is important to note that, just like the **While** loop, the **Do-While** loop does not increment a counter or change the logical expression automatically. You must increment your own counter or make sure the logical expression can change within the loop.

 "For" loops will automatically increase the index after each loop, and will exit the loop when this index reaches the target number. "While" loops and "Do-While" loops do NOT do this automatically. If you do not change the logical expression within your loop, the loop could execute forever! This is what is called an "infinite" loop.

A bottom-tested **Do-While** loop looks like this:

```
Do
        ' statements to execute
Loop While (condition)
```

The first line just tells the program that we are going to start our **Do** loop. The next line(s) contain the code that we want to execute within our loop. The last line is where the program will test the logical expression, and if **True**, continue executing the statements starting at the top of the **Do** loop again. Let's rewrite our 5-count example using a **Do-While** loop:

```
Dim loopCounter As Integer = 0
Do
        MsgBox("We are now at loop number: " & loopCounter )
        loopCounter = loopCounter + 1
Loop While loopCounter < 5
```

Remember that the loop-condition will not be tested until after the loop has already executed once, so we will run the loop statements at least one time. Don't forget to initialize the **loopCounter** variable before entering the loop!

Lesson Three: Using Loops in a Program

Now that we know what a loop looks like, let's try one in a program! Open the Visual Basic IDE and create a project called "Loops". Click on the form and change the **(Name)** property to "LoopForm" and the **Text** property to "Looping Around".

In this program, we will create a form that has two buttons. We will have a button to run a **For** loop and a button to run a **While** loop.

Go ahead and create two buttons on your form. Change your **(Name)** and **Text** properties to:

- Button1: **(Name)** = "ForButton" and **Text** = "For Loop"
- Button2: **(Name)** = "WhileButton" and **Text** = "While Loop"

Your form should now look like this:

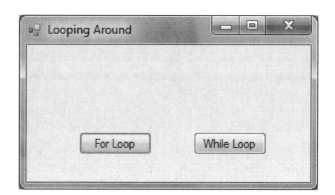

Now we will create the code for our buttons. Each time the user clicks a button, we want the program to ask the user for a number, and then run a **For** or **While** loop that number of times. Each time through the loop we'll have the computer make a short beeping sound. That way you can count the beeps to make sure your loops are executing the right number of times!

We will use the **Console.Beep()** function to make some noise. Each time you call the **Console.Beep()** function your computer should make a brief sound through your computer speakers.

 **Some computers may not have the right hardware to make any noise when you use Console.Beep()! If you call Console.Beep() and don't hear anything, try replacing that line with a simple MsgBox() instead. That way you can still count the number of loops and don't have to worry about the sound.**

Each button should ask the user how many times they want the computer to beep, and then use this value to create a loop. We'll start with the "For Loop" button.

Double-click on the "For Loop" button to bring up the code window for the button's event handler function. The first thing we need to do is create two **Integer** variables: one to hold the number of times the user wants to beep and one to hold the current index number in our **For** loop:

```
Dim beepNumber As Integer
Dim currentIndex As Integer
```

Now let's ask the user how many times they want to beep, and convert the input text to a number:

```
beepNumber = Val(InputBox("How many times do you want to beep?", _
                "Beep Question"))
```

Finally, we need to set up our **For** loop:

```
For currentIndex = 1 To beepNumber
     Console.Beep()
Next
```

We will loop from 1 up to the number that our user has entered ("**beepNumber**"). We don't need to use the **Step** keyword, since we want to count by 1 and 1 is the default **Step**.

Now run your program and see what happens! Try entering different values for the beep number.

Next, we will add the code for our **While** loop. Double-click on the "While Loop" button to bring up the code window. This code will look very similar to the **For** loop. Start by declaring your variables and getting the number of beeps from the user:

```
Dim beepNumber As Integer
Dim currentIndex As Integer

beepNumber = Val(InputBox("How many times do you want to beep?", _
                "Beep Question"))
```

Now we will create our **While** Loop. Notice that we must first initialize our **currentIndex** variable!

```
currentIndex = 0
While currentIndex < beepNumber
    Console.Beep()
    currentIndex = currentIndex + 1
End While
```

Our **While** loop will continue as long as the **currentIndex** is less than the number of times the user wants to beep. The most important line in the **While** loop is the third line: "**currentIndex = currentIndex + 1**". This increments the **currentIndex** variable, so the **While** condition will eventually become **False**. If you accidentally forgot this line, your program will make the computer beep forever!

Make sure you remember to save your project when you close the application. To do this, click on "File" and "Close Project". Name your project "Loops", make sure you are saving in your "C:\KidCoder\Windows Programming\My Projects" directory, and name your solution "Loops".

Chapter Review

- A **For** loop is used to repeat a set of code statements a certain number of times.

- The **For** loop is based on an index variable that is increased each time through the loop.

- A **While** loop is used to repeat a set of code statements while a condition is **True**.

- A **While** loop's logical expression must eventually evaluate to **False** or else you will be stuck in an infinite loop.

- A **Do-While** loop is very similar to a **While** loop but the condition is tested at the bottom, so the loop will always execute at least once.

- A **Do-While** loop's logical expressions must eventually evaluate to **False** in order to terminate the loop or else you will be stuck in an infinite loop.

Your Turn: Getting Loopy

In this activity, you will add a bottom-tested **Do-While** loop to "Loops" project you create in this chapter.

Open the "Loops" project you created in the last lesson. To do this, open up the Visual Basic IDE and click on "File" and "Open Project". Your project should have been saved in "C:\KidCoder\Windows Programming\My Projects\Loops" and the filename should be "Loops.sln". Select this file to open the project. If you do not see your project's screen and code, just use the icons on the Solution Explorer to show the screens.

Now you are going to add a new button and code to use a **Do-While** loop:

- Add a button called "DoWhileButton" and with the text: "Do While Loop"
- Double-click the button to create the button's event handler function
- Create an **Integer** variable called **beepNumber**
- Create an **Integer** variable called **currentIndex**
- Use an **InputBox()** to ask the user how many times they want to make the computer beep
- Write a bottom-tested **Do-While** loop that will loop the right number of times
  - Inside the loop, use the **Console.Beep()** function to make the computer beep
  - Don't forget to initialize the **currentIndex** before the loop starts and add one to it within the loop

Here is your form with the new button added:

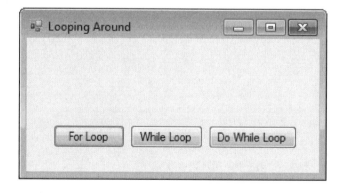

When you run the program your new button should make the computer beep the number of times requested by the user!

Chapter Eleven: Functions

A *function* is a set of statements that can be used over and over again from different places in your program. Some functions such as **MsgBox()** are pre-made for you, while others you can write yourself. This chapter is all about writing and using your own functions!

Lesson One: Writing Subs and Functions

Functions have two forms in Visual Basic: **Function** and **Sub**. "Sub" is short for "subroutine". A **function** or **Sub** is a group of program statements that perform some job. The only difference between a **Function** and a **Sub** is that functions return a value and subroutines do not return anything. In this textbook we may generally say just "function" when talking about both functions and subroutines. Where we need to talk about a **Function** or **Sub** individually, those names will be in bold print.

Let's think back to some of the **Functions** that we have used in this course. Here are some examples:

```
IsNumeric()
Strings.Left()
InputBox()
```

All of these functions returned a value to us when they were finished executing.

We have also used this **Sub**:

```
Console.Beep()
```

All of our button click event handlers are also subroutines. None of these subroutines returned a value when they were finished.

Private vs. Public

Functions can be created as either **Public** or **Private**. **Public** functions can be used anywhere in our program. You could also use the word **Private**, which means that the function can only be used in one specific area of our program. For example, a **Private** function can only be used on the Form where it was written.

When you create code for a button-click event, you may notice that the **Sub** for the event looks something like this:

```
    Private Sub Button1_Click.........


End Sub
```

This is a **Private** subroutine since the "Button-Click" event can only be called by the form that contains the button. All of our projects in this course have only one form, so it doesn't matter if you use **Public** or **Private** for your functions; each function can still be called from anywhere in the form. We will usually pick **Public** for our examples.

Writing Your Own Subs

A **Sub** has the following format:

```
    Public Sub SubName()
         ' statements
End Sub
```

The first word, **Public**, tells us that this subroutine is available for use throughout our program. The second word is the **Sub** keyword. This keyword tells the program that we are creating a subroutine, or **Sub**. The next word is the name of your **Sub**. This should be a meaningful name that describes what the **Sub** will do. The rules for subroutine names are basically the same as the rules for naming a variable! The open and closing parenthesis () may contain parameters or input data; these will be described later.

The last line is **End Sub**. This line tells the program that we have finished our subroutine. The line(s) between the lines **Public Sub** and **End Sub** are where you put the code statements that will run when the **Sub** is called.

Say we want to create a **Sub** that displays **MsgBox**() with the current date and time. Here's how we do it:

```
    Public Sub DateTimeMsgBox()
        MsgBox(DateTime.Now)
End Sub
```

Our **Sub** is called "DateTimeMsgBox" and has just one line of code: "**MsgBox(DateTime.Now)**". You can use the phrase "**DateTime.Now**" to easily get the current date and time from your computer. **DateTime** is a Visual Basic data type that can hold any date and time value. The **Now** property will always give you the current time.

Writing Your Own Functions

A **Function** has the following format:

```
Public Function FunctionName() As Data type
    ' statements
End Function
```

The **Function** keyword tells the Visual Basic that we will be creating a new function. The next word is the name of your function. This should be a meaningful name that describes what the function will do and should follow standard variable naming rules. Just like a **Sub**, a **Function** can also have input data inside the parenthesis (), and we'll describe that later. The last item on the first line is "**As** data type". This is where you describe the return value for your **Function**. A return value is data that is passed back to the calling code after the **Function** is finished. The data type can be anything Visual Basic understands as data like an **Integer**, **String**, or even a **DateTime**!

The last line in the function is **End Function**. This tells the program that we have finished our function. The line(s) between **Public Function** and **End Function** are where you put the code statements that the function will execute when called.

Let's say that we want to create a **Function** that will return the current date and time as a string. Here is an example of how that function could be written:

```
Public Function GetCurrentDate() As String
    Dim currentDate As String = DateTime.Now.ToString()
    Return currentDate
End Function
```

Our **Function** is called "GetCurrentDate" and returns a **String** when it is finished. The function statements will create a **String** variable called **currentDate**. The variable is initialized by calling the **ToString()** function on **DateTime.Now**, which will take the current time and change it to a String. Finally the **Return** statement will return that value to the piece of code that called the function.

 Functions and subs are very similar, with one main difference: A function will always return a value to the program. A sub never returns a value to the program.

Lesson Two: Parameters for Subs and Functions

The functions and subroutines we created in the last lesson were very simple. The program calls them and they perform a quick and easy task. But what if we wanted to do a more complicated or useful task? We can add *input parameters* to a function to give it some data to work with.

Parameters are values that are passed or shared into a function. These values can then be used by the statements within to do some work.

Sub Parameters

The format for a **Sub** with parameters looks like this:

```
Public Sub SubName(ByVal parameter1 As data type1, _
                   ByVal parameter2 As data type2)
      ' statements
End Sub
```

This format is the same as the normal **Sub**, but contains a list of parameters between the parentheses. A subroutine can have as many parameters as you wish. If you have more than one parameter, the different values are separated by a comma.

Each parameter is declared just like a normal variable, without the **Dim** statement. The first parameter above is "parameter1 **As** data type1". The "parameter1" is the name for your parameter, and can be any valid variable name. The data type represents the type of data that you are giving to your subroutine. The **ByVal** keyword will be added by the Visual Basic IDE automatically so we don't usually show it in our examples. **ByVal** means that a copy of the input parameter will be handed to the **Function** or **Sub** to use. The **Function** or **Sub** cannot change the original data passed into the function when using **ByVal**!

Let's say we wanted to print out a "hello" message to a specific person. We could pass the person's name into a **Sub** and use the **MsgBox()** function to pop-up our message:

```
Public Sub HelloMsgBox(personName As String)
      MsgBox("Hello " & personName)
End Sub
```

This **Sub** has only one line: "**MsgBox**("Hello " & personName)". This line calls the **MsgBox()** function and prints out a message with the **personName** parameter that was passed into the subroutine. Statements inside a function or subroutine can use the input parameters just like any other variable, but any changes to the variable made within the function won't be seen outside the function!

Function Parameters

The format for a **Function** with parameters looks like this:

```
Public Function FunctionName(parameter1 As data type1, …)  As data type
     ' statements
End Function
```

This format is the same as the normal **Function**, but contains a list of parameters in between the parentheses. The rules and format for **Function** parameters are the same as **Sub** parameters! A function can have as many parameters as you wish. If you have more than one parameter, the different values are separated by a comma. Just like **Sub** parameters, each **Function** parameter is declared by giving it a variable name and data type.

Let's say that we wanted to create a **Function** that will find the higher of two input numbers. We would need to create parameters to pass in the two numbers that will be compared:

```
Public Function FindMax(number1 As Integer, number2 As Integer) _
                                                As Integer
        If (number1 > number2)
             Return number1
        End If
        Return number2
End Function
```

In this example, the **FindMax()** function takes two **Integer** parameters named **number1** and **number2**. It returns an **Integer** result. The **If** statement will return the first number if it is higher. Otherwise we just return the second number.

Lesson Three: Calling Subs and Functions

So far in this chapter we have covered how to create **Functions** and **Subs**, how to give input parameters and return values from **Functions**. Now we will see how to use or *call* functions in a program.

Calling Subs and Functions without Parameters

You have already learned how to use many subroutines and functions such as **MsgBox()**. To call or run a function, you simply write the function name with opening and closing parenthesis () like this:

```
FunctionName()
```

Pretty simple, right? You can call both a **Sub** and a **Function** in this way. If your function does not need any input parameters, then there is nothing between the parentheses ().

Using Function Return Values

Remember that a **Function** will always return a data value. If you simply call the **Function** on a separate line, as shown above, then the returned data is lost! That might be ok if you don't need the data. But if you want to save the return value, you need to call the **Function** within an assignment statement, and save the return data in some variable!

```
returnValue = FunctionName()
```

The **returnValue** must be a variable that has been declared with the same type as your function's return data type. For example, earlier we created a sample function called **GetCurrentDate()** that returns a **String** value. To call this function, we need to create a **String** variable to handle that return value:

```
Dim returnValue As String
returnValue = GetCurrentDate()
```

When the function is finished a string with the current date and time would be placed into the variable **returnValue**.

You can also place function calls in larger expressions, using the returned data as part of a larger calculation or logical expression. Here we call the **Abs()** method to get a numeric result, and then compare it to another number:

```
Dim inputValue As Integer = -3
If (Abs(inputValue) > 2) Then
    ' do something here
End If
```

Just remember that a **Function's** returned data type must be a good match for what you are trying to do. Don't call a **Function** that returns a **String** and then try to do some math on it! As you might expect, you cannot use a **Sub** as part of a larger expression, because there is no return data!

Calling Subs and Functions with Parameters

Calling functions with parameters is very similar to calling those without parameters. The only difference is that we have to pass in variables or values that match the function's parameter list. A call to a function with parameters would look like this:

```
FunctionName(parameter1, parameter2,…)
```

For instance, earlier we created a **Sub** that displayed a **MsgBox**() with a person's name in it. To use that **Sub**, we would make a call with one string input parameter. This call passes the string value "Alice" into our **Sub**:

```
HelloMsgBox("Alice")
```

Calling a **Function** with parameters is done exactly the same way! Remember, earlier we created a **Function** that found the higher of two numbers. Let's use the function:

```
Dim firstNumber As Integer = 27
Dim result As Integer = FindMax(firstNumber, 42)
```

In this example we created a variable to hold the **Integer** result of our function. We also created an **Integer** variable `firstNumber` to hold one of our input numbers. The function call passes the variable `firstNumber` and the number 42 to our function. You can pass either variables or values to functions, as long as you are passing the correct type of data. After the function call returns, the value 42 would be stored in the `result` because that number is bigger than the 27 stored in `firstNumber`.

Ordering of Parameters

When you are calling functions with parameters the *order* of the parameters is important! Variables or data must be passed into the function in the order that they were listed in the function description.

For instance, consider the following **Sub** with three parameters:

```
Public Sub PrintAddress(city As String, state As String, _
                        zip As Integer)
```

When you call the **Sub** you must pass in data in the order: "`city`", "`state`", and "`zip`". Visual Basic will assume that the first parameter in your calling statement will go to the first variable in the parameter list; the second parameter in the calling statement will go to the second variable in the parameter list, and so on. You cannot pass in the state first and the city last, for example, and have the data received correctly by the function.

The names of the variables that you pass to a function do not matter; only the ordering and data type are important. For example, if you declared a **Sub** with parameters called **base** and **height**:

```
Public Sub CalculateTriangleArea(base As Integer, height As Integer)
```

You can call the **Sub** with any two variable parameters, as long as they are **Integers**. The names do not have to match:

```
CalculateTriangleArea(myBase, myHeight)
```

The names of your parameters do not matter when calling a function or subroutine. The order of the parameters, however, is extremely important! If the function needs an Integer and then a String, you cannot pass a String and then an Integer. You must pass the parameters in the order that the function is expecting.

Lesson Four: Writing Your Own Function

In this lesson, we will create our own function to compute the area of a rectangle. First, go ahead and create a new project in the Visual Basic IDE called "Functions". Once this project is created, change the Form **(Name)** to "FunctionForm" and the **Text** to "Functions".

The area of a rectangle is equal to its length multiplied by width. We will need to create two textboxes where a user can type in these values. We will also need labels to tell the user what to type in each textbox. Go ahead and add two textboxes and two descriptive labels to your form. Change the textbox **(Name)** properties to "**LengthTextBox**" and "**WidthTexBox**". Here is an example of your form so far:

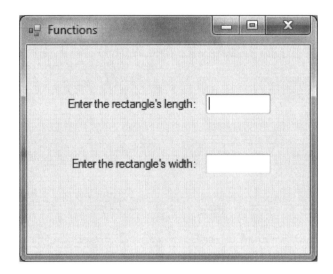

Now add a button that the user can use to compute the area of their rectangle. Change the button's **(Name)** to "RectAreaButton" and the **Text** to "Rectangle Area". Your form should now look like this:

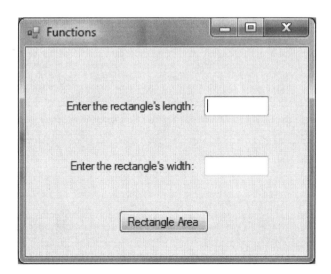

Now, click on the "View Code" button to view the code window for our form. You should see the following code in your source file:

```
    Public Class FunctionForm


    End Class
```

We will add our function between these two lines because it belongs to our "FunctionForm"! Since our function will compute the area of a rectangle, we will call it **ComputeRectArea()**. We will be using two **Integer** parameters for the length and width of the rectangle and an **Integer** return value to return the area back to our program.

Begin by typing in our function declaration like this:

```
    Public Function ComputeRectArea(ByVal rectLength As Integer, _
                             ByVal rectWidth As Integer) As Integer
```

As soon as you hit the "Enter" key after this statement, the code window should add the **End Function** statement a few lines below our first **Function** statement. The code for our function will go between these lines.

We will now add the code for the body of the function. All we need this function to do is multiply the **rectLength** times the **rectWidth** and return the answer to the user. This can be done with the following line:

```
    Return rectLength * rectWidth
```

That's it! The final function should look like this:

```
    Public Function ComputeRectArea(ByVal rectLength As Integer, _
                             ByVal rectWidth As Integer) As Integer
        Return rectLength * rectWidth
    End Function
```

Now we need to add some code to make the button on our form call our function. To do this, go back to the form view and double-click on the "Rectangle Area" button. This will bring up our code window with the button's event handler function.

Within the button function, first add an **Integer** variable to hold the return value from our function:

```
    Dim rectArea As Integer
```

Next we need to get the values out of each text box, convert the strings to numbers, pass the numbers into our **ComputeRectArea**() function, and store the returned data into our variable. We can do all of that in one line:

```
rectArea = ComputeRectArea(Val( LengthTextBox.Text ), _
                           Val( WidthTextBox.Text ))
```

Notice that we are using the **Val**() function to change the string contents of our textboxes to the numeric data that our function is expecting.

Finally, we will use a **MsgBox**() function to display the result to the user:

```
MsgBox ("The area of your rectangle is: " & rectArea)
```

Our final button code should look like this:

```
Private Sub RectAreaButton_Click(ByVal sender As System.Object, _
                                 ByVal e As System.EventArgs)   _
                                 Handles RectAreaButton.Click
    Dim rectArea As Integer
    rectArea = ComputeRectArea(Val(LengthTextBox.Text), _
                               Val(WidthTextBox.Text))
    MsgBox("Your rectangle's area is: " & rectArea)
End Sub
```

Now run your program and try some different input values. Do you get the right answer?

Make sure you remember to save your project when you close the application. To do this, click on "File" and "Close Project". Name your project "Functions", make sure you are saving in your "C:\KidCoder\Windows Programming\My Projects" directory, and name your solution "Functions".

 **Chapter Review**

- A *function* is a collection of code that performs a specific task.

- There are two types of functions in Visual Basic: **Function** and **Sub**.

- A **Function** always returns a value to the statement that called it.

- A **Sub** never returns a value to the statement that called it.

- A *return value* is a piece of information that a **Function** can give back to the calling code.

- A *parameter* is a piece of information that a program can share with a **Function** or **Sub**.

- A **Function** is usually called from an assignment statement to store the return data in a variable.

- Functions can also be used in larger expressions if they return the correct data type.

- You can name a **Function** or **Sub** anything that follows the standard variable naming rules.

- The names of parameters in a **Function** or **Sub** are not important, but the order and data types of these parameters are extremely important.

Your Turn: Zip Zap Latin

In this activity, we will create a new program based on our Pig Latin program from Chapter 8. Our new program will use a function to translate a word, and will allow us to change the "way" and "ay" Pig Latin endings into new endings the user can choose.

Open up the Visual Basic IDE and create a new project called "Zippy Functions". Click on the Form and change the **(Name)** to "ZipZapForm" and the **Text** to "Zip Zap Latin".

Now you will need to do the following:

- Add a textbox control with the **(Name)** "WordTextBox" and a **Label** "Enter a word:"
- Add a textbox control with the **(Name)** "TranslateTextBox" and a **Label** "Translated word:"
- Add a button control with the **(Name)** "ZipButton" and the **Text**: "Zip Latin"
- Add a button control with the **(Name)** "ZapButton" and the **Text**: "Zap Latin"

At this point, your form should look something like this:

![Zip Zap Latin form with Enter your word and Translated word textboxes, and ZAP Latin and ZIP Latin buttons]

Now you are going to write a function that will change the user's word into a new form of Pig Latin!

To do this, click on "View Code" or press F7 to bring up the code window. You will add your function after the line "**Public Class** ZipZapForm". The function declaration will look like this:

```
Public Function Translator(ByVal vowelPhrase As String, _
                   ByVal consonantPhrase As String, _
                   ByVal word As String) As String
```

Your function will take 3 **String** parameters:

- **vowelPhrase** —the string that we will add to the end if the word starts with a vowel
- **consonantPhrase** – the string that we will add to the end if the word starts with a consonant
- **word** – the word to be translated

The function will return a **String** value which holds the translated word. Now, inside your **Translator** function you should do the following:

- Translate the **word** parameter into all lower-case characters to make looking for the vowels easier
- Create a **Char** variable called **firstCharacter**, and set it equal to the first character of the **word** variable (remember the string functions you learned earlier?)
- Create a **String** variable called **resultString**, which will hold the translated word
- Create an **Integer** variable called **stringLength**, and set it equal to the length of the **word** variable that was passed into our function
- If the **firstCharacter** is an "a", "e", "i", "o", or "u", then set the **resultString** equal to the **word** with a dash "-" and the **vowelPhrase** added to the end
- Otherwise, then set the **resultString** equal to the **word** (without the first letter) with a dash "-", then the **firstCharacter** and finally the **consonantPhrase**
- At the end of the function, return the **returnString** value

Note: This function is almost a direct copy of the "TranslateButton_Click" method in your earlier Pig Latin Translator program. If you get stuck, take a look at that earlier code to see how we did it!

Now that you have your function, you need to call it when the **ZipButton** and **ZapButton** are clicked:

- When the **ZapButton** is clicked, call the **Translator** function with "zap" as the vowel phrase, "ap" as the consonant phrase, and the contents of the **WordTextBox** as the word to be translated.
  - o Save the results into the **TranslateTextBox** so the user can see the translated word
- When the **ZipButton** is clicked, call the **Translator** function with "zip" as the vowel phrase, "ip" as the consonant phrase, and the contents of the **WordTextBox** as the word to be translated.
  - o Save the results into the **TranslateTextBox** so the user can see the translated word

Run your program and test both buttons! Here are some examples:

- "hello" translates to "ello-hap" with the Zap button and "ello-hip" with the Zip button
- "apple" translates to "apple-zap" with the Zap button and "apple-zip" with the Zip button

Chapter Twelve: Arrays and Structures

So far you have used variables that each holds one piece of data. In this chapter we will study the concepts of arrays and structures, which allow you to hold much more data using one variable name.

Lesson One: Simple Arrays

Earlier we showed how to use the **Dim** statement to create variables. The variables that we created were all individual variables, meaning each variable name held one piece of data. If we needed to create a variable to hold a student's grade, we might have used the following code:

```
Dim studentGrade As Integer
```

If we needed to create variables to hold the grades of 10 students, we could create 10 different variables:

```
Dim student1Grade As Integer
Dim student2Grade As Integer
.
.
.
Dim student10Grade As Integer
```

However, this would take a long time and many lines of code. Imagine what we would have to do if we had a hundred students!

Instead, we can create a set of data represented by one variable name. This group of data is called an *array*. Arrays make using groups of one data type very simple. You can create an array of any data type in Visual Basic. You can have an array of integers, strings, or other data types.

Here is how we would declare an array of 10 integers for students' grades:

```
Dim studentGrade(9) As Integer
```

This looks a lot like our normal integer declaration. The only difference is the number in parentheses after the variable name. This line creates an array, or group of 10 integer variables. Each of the variables in an array is called an *element* and each element can be accessed by its element number, which is called an *index*.

You will probably notice that we use the number 9 instead of 10 in our declaration. This is not a mistake! Arrays in Visual Basic are zero-based. This means that the first element is **not** number 1, it is number 0. Our example above created an array of 10 integers – element 0, element 1, element 2, element 3, element 4, element 5, element 6, element 7, element 8, and element 9.

 One of the most frequent errors when using arrays is to forget that they are zero-based. The first element of an array is always index 0, NOT index 1!

Each element in the array is named by its index value in parentheses. So to use the first element in the array, we could use the following code:

```
studentGrade(0) = 95
```

This would set the value of the first **studentGrade** integer to 95. To set the value of the 4th student's grade, we would do the following:

```
studentGrade(3) = 84
```

Again, notice that because we start the index at 0, the 4th student's grade is kept in **studentGrade**(3) and not **studentGrade**(4).

You can also declare and initialize an array at the same time. If we knew our 10 student's grades ahead of time, we could use the following line to declare our array and set the values:

```
Dim studentGrade() As Integer = {90, 95, 80, 85, 93, 92, 88, 75, 90, 80}
```

This one line of code will create an array of integers that has 10 elements. The value of element 0 is set to 90, element 1 is set to 95, and so on. Do not set the array size in parenthesis when providing a list of values!

If we need to read the information from elements in an array, use the same index values. Here we take a couple of elements from the array and use them to show messages in a **MsgBox**:

```
MsgBox("The 1st student's grade is: " & studentGrade(0) )
MsgBox("The 4th student's grade is: " & studentGrade(3) )
```

Again, it is important to remember that our arrays are zero-based! If you tried to access element 10 in the array, like this:

```
MsgBox("The 10th student's grade is: " & studentGrade(10) )
```

You would get an error, since the array only has elements 0 – 9. Element number 10 does not exist. The program would immediately give you an error window with the message: "Index out of bounds", which means the index that you tried to use was outside the end of your array. This is a common mistake when programming with arrays.

The number of elements in the array is also called the "length" of the array. Our example 10-element student grade array has a length of 10. Now, how do we find out the length of an array if you do not already know it? To find the length of an array, you can simply read the array's **Length** property. Given our example **studentGrade** array, here's how to read the **Length** property:

```
Dim lengthOfArray As Integer = studentGrade.Length
```

Many times you will want to use all of the items in an array. Let's say you wanted to print out a list of all of the students and their grades. You will need to print out each element of the array, one at a time. The most common way to do this is to use a **For** loop, like this:

```
Dim studentGrade() As Integer = {90, 95, 80, 85, 93, 92, 88, 75, 90, 80}
Dim lengthOfArray As Integer = studentGrade.Length

Dim i As Integer
For i = 0 To lengthOfArray - 1
    'Your print statement here
Next
```

Let's take a closer look at the **For** statement above: First, you will notice that we will start our loop at 0. Again, this is because the first array index starts at 0, not 1. Then we will loop to "**lengthOfArray** – 1". Why minus 1? This is because the last element in an array is always the length of the array minus 1. So, the last element in a 10-element array is element 9 (10 – 1), the last element in a 3-element array is element 2 (3 – 1), and the last element in a 5-element array is 4 (5 – 1).

You don't have to declare a separate **lengthOfArray** variable if you don't want to. You can use the **Length** property directly in your **For** loop:

```
For i = 0 To studentGrade.Length - 1
```

By using the **Length** property directly in your **For** loop, you can be sure you are going to loop over each of the elements in the array and stop at exactly the right index, no matter what the actual array size may be! The following loop will show a **MsgBox** for each student's grade.

```
For i = 0 To studentGrade.Length - 1
    MsgBox("Student Grade: " & studentGrade(i))
Next
```

ReDim Arrays

You may need to change the size of an array in the middle of a program. Maybe you don't know how many students are in a class when the program starts! You could ask the user to tell you how many students they want to process. In this case, you will need to **ReDim** your array. A **ReDim** will allow you to re-state how many items that you want the array to hold. For example, let's say you create an initial **studentGrade** array of 10 items:

```
Dim studentGrade(9) As Integer
```

Then, the user decides that they actually need to process 15 students. Here is where the **ReDim** becomes useful:

```
ReDim studentGrade(14)
```

Note that if you want to create an array with one element, you would use **ReDim studentGrade**(0). You can even create an array with no elements at all by using **ReDim studentGrade**(-1)!

The **ReDim** statement by itself will erase all of the data that is contained in this array. So this statement is only useful before you put data into the array. But what if you do already have data in the array that you want to save? Then you can use the **ReDim Preserve** statement:

```
ReDim Preserve studentGrade(14)
```

This will re-size the array AND will keep all the existing data in the original elements. There is no loss of data when you use the keyword **Preserve**, unless you **ReDim** to a smaller size than the first array.

Lesson Two: Two-Dimensional Arrays

Let's take a look at our student grade example one more time. This time, we need to hold the grades for three different exams for our 10 students. Our information will look something like this:

	Exam 1 Grade	Exam 2 Grade	Exam 3 Grade
Student 1	85	93	76
Student 2	87	85	83
…	…	…	…
Student 10	92	75	85

In this simple data grid we have one row for each student and one column for each exam grade. It would be hard to hold this data as a one-dimensional array (an array with only one row or column). We could create three different arrays (one for each exam) to hold this information, but that would take a lot of work. Instead, we will use a two-dimensional array to hold this data.

So far, the arrays that we have been talking about are one-dimensional; they have only one index. These arrays are often thought of as a single list of elements, like a stack of paper. A two-dimensional array can be thought of as a grid of data, where each element in the array is one cell in the grid. If you take a look at the grid above, you will see that each shaded block in the grid has a row and a column. The first row holds the grades for "Student 1", the second holds the grades for "Student 2", etc. The first column has the grades from the first exam; the second column has the grades for the second exam, and so on.

We can label each of the shaded blocks by using their row and column number. For example, using zero-based indexing, the first student's grade for the first exam is located at row 0, column 0. The second student's grade for the third exam is located at row 1, column 2.

We can easily represent data grids as two-dimensional arrays in code. To declare a two-dimensional array, just add a second number to the **Dim** statement:

```
Dim StudentGrades(2,9) As Integer
```

This creates a two dimensional array that has 3 columns (0 – 2) and 10 rows (0 – 9). To set the first student's grade for the first exam, we would use the following code:

```
StudentGrades(0,0) = 85
```

Notice that the first row and column in an array is 0 and not 1. You have probably already figured out how to set the second student's grade for the third exam:

```
        StudentGrades(2,1) = 83
```

Reading the data from the two-dimensional array is similar:

```
        myGrade = StudentGrades(2,3)
```

This would set the value of **myGrade** equal to the fourth student's grade for the third exam.

Lesson Three: Structures

In this course we have used many different kinds of built-in data types. These data types have allowed us to define variables that hold decimal numbers, whole numbers, strings and date/time values. In this lesson we will learn how to create our *own* data types that hold more than one of the built-in data types.

Why would you need to create your own data type? There are often cases where you have several pieces of data that should be grouped together. For example, let's consider a person's mailing address. In the USA an address is a combination of a street address, a city, a state and a zip code. We could declare a variable to hold each part of the address like this:

```
    Dim streetAddress As String
    Dim cityAddress As String
    Dim stateAddress As String
    Dim zipAddress As Integer
```

These variables will work just fine, but what if we wanted to track more than one mailing address at the same time? We wouldn't want to declare streetAddress1, streetAddress2, etc. What we'd like to do is declare variables of an **Address** data type, where the **Address** contains all of the individual elements needed to hold a mailing address.

We can do this with a *data structure* in Visual Basic. A structure allows us to group data together into a new, single data type. To define a new data type in Visual Basic, use the **Structure** keyword like this:

```
    Public Structure Address
        Dim street As String
        Dim city As String
        Dim state As String
        Dim zip As Integer
    End Structure
```

The opening **Structure** statement is followed by your new name for the structure data type, in this case: **Address**. The **Dim** statements inside of the structure define the variables we want to group together in the structure. The **End Structure** statement tells Visual Basic that the data structure has ended.

Once you have defined a new structure, you can create a variable of that new data type:

```
Dim myAddress As Address
```

When we need to assign values to the elements in the **Address** data structure, we use the dot (.) just like using a property from a textbox or other control:

```
myAddress.street = "123 Peachtree Street"
myAddress.city = "Atlanta"
myAddress.state = "GA"
myAddress.zip = 30113
```

We can read these values the same way:

```
MsgBox ("My street is: " & myAddress.street)
```

 **The dot (.) operator is a very important part of Visual Basic syntax. This operator is used to get and set properties and call functions on objects.**

There are some special rules to remember when dealing with structures in Visual Basic. First, you can initialize the variables in a structure definition or after you declare a variable of that type. Any elements initialized in the structure definition will set the default values when structure variables are declared.

```
Public Structure Glass
    Dim isHalfFull As Boolean = True
    Dim isHalfEmpty As Boolean = False
End Structure
```

Now when you **Dim** a variable of type **Glass**, the **isHalfFull** and **isHalfEmpty** elements are already set to the values chosen above. You can, of course, set the elements to any other values you like after you **Dim** the variable.

```
Dim myGlass As Glass
myGlass.isHalfFull = False
```

It is important to remember to initialize all of the variables in a structure (either in the definition or after declaring the variable) before you use the variable in your program!

Using Arrays in Structures

You can also have arrays inside a data structure. Arrays have a special set of rules when they are used in a structure, however. You cannot declare the dimension of an array inside of the structure definition. To explain this in an example, let's take a look at our **Address** structure. A person often has a two-line street address. For this reason, we decide to declare the street variable as a two-element **String** array:

```
Public Structure Address
        Dim street() As String
        Dim city As String
        Dim state As String
        Dim zip As Integer
End Structure
```

Notice that we defined the **street** variable as a **String** array, but did not set the size of the array. This must be done after you create the variable by using the **ReDim** statement:

```
Dim myAddress As Address
ReDim myAddress.street(1)
```

Now we can use the **street** array like any other array:

```
myAddress.street(0) = "123 Business Drive"
myAddress.street(1) = "Suite 104"
```

 **It is very important to remember the ReDim step when you are using arrays within structures.**

Arrays of Structures

Just as you can have an array of any other data type, it is possible (and often useful) to have an array of structures. In our **Address** structure example, we could use an array of **Addresses** to create an entire **Address** book. You declare an array of structures like other arrays:

```
Dim myAddressBook(9) As Address
```

Now we can hold 10 Addresses in our **myAddressBook** array! Let's take a look at a fancy example that will create an address book and fill out all 10 entries.

```
' first declare the address book and a loop counter variable
Dim myAddressBook(9) As Address
Dim i As Integer


' now loop over all structures in the array
For i = 0 To myAddressBook.Length - 1

    ' make sure to ReDim the array within our structure
    ReDim myAddressBook(i).street(1)

    ' now fill out all of the variables in the structure!

    myAddressBook(i).street(0) = "First street # " & i
    myAddressBook(i).street(1) = "Second street # " & i
    myAddressBook(i).city = "City # " & i
    myAddressBook(i).state = "State # " & i
    myAddressBook(i).zip = 30000 + i
Next
```

What's going on here? The first task is to declare our array of structures. We'll be using a **For** loop to fill out each one of the array structures, so we declare a counter variable "**i**". Next we start the **For** loop, going from "0" to the "length of the array - 1" so we cover all 10 elements with indexes 0 through 9.

Within the loop we first **ReDim** the **street** array for the structure we're looking at. Then we fill out each of the elements in the structure with some fake data. After completing the loop the first **Address** element in the address book, **myAddressBook**(0), will have this data:

> **street**(0) = "First street # 0"
> **street**(1) = "Second street # 0"
> **city** = "City # 0"
> **state** = "State # 0"
> **zip** = 30000

The second element **myAddressBook**(1) will have:
> **street**(0) = "First street # 1"
> **street**(1) = "Second street # 1"
> **city** = "City # 1"
> **state** = "State # 1"
> **zip** = 30001

…and so on!

Lesson Four: Using Structures and Arrays in a Program

In this lesson, we are going to put our structures and arrays to work in an actual program. To do this, we are going to be creating a "Piggy Bank" program. We will put money into the bank or take money out of the bank using a "Transaction". Each **Transaction** will contain a dollar amount and a date for the deposit or withdrawal. We will use an array of **Transactions** to keep track of the money in the bank.

The first thing we need to do is create our project and our main form. To do this, open the Visual Basic IDE and create a new project called "Piggy Bank". Set the form **(Name)** to "BankForm" and the **Text** to "Bank of Oink". Then add the following controls to our form:

- A label control with the text "Enter amount:"
- A NumericUpDown control with a **(Name)** of "dollarAmount"
- A button control with a **(Name)** of "DepositButton" and the **Text**: "Deposit"
- A button control with a **(Name)** of "WithdrawalButton" and the **Text**: "Withdraw"

Now your form should look something like this:

Let's start adding some code! The first piece of code that we will write is our **Transaction** structure. Go ahead and open up the code window by clicking on "View Code" or by pressing the F7 key. Add our structure just under the line "**Public Class** BankForm":

```
Public Structure Transaction
        Dim amount As Decimal
        Dim time As Date
End Structure
```

As you can see, we have named our structure **Transaction** and given it two elements: a **Decimal** value called **amount** and a **Date** value called **time**. This will allow us to keep track of how much money the user has deposited or withdrawn and what time the transaction took place.

Now we need to add a **Transaction** array that will hold our user's piggy bank deposits and withdrawals:

```
Dim transactions(-1) As Transaction
```

Notice that we are creating an array with a top index of "-1". This means that the array will begin with a length of 0. We will add new transactions to the array as the user adds and subtracts money from their bank.

Next, before we add any code to the buttons, we are going to create a helper function. This function will be called **addTransaction** and it will be used to deposit money (add a positive value to the bank) or withdraw money (add a negative value to the bank). Once this function is done, we can use it from our button clicks.

Underneath your **Transaction** structure definition, declare a new **addTransaction** subroutine like this:

```
Private Sub addTransaction(ByVal dollarAmount As Decimal)
```

As you can see, our subroutine takes in one parameter: a **Decimal** dollar amount, and does not return any value. Now we can add some code to this function. First, add an **Integer** variable that will hold the starting length of the transactions array:

```
Dim i As Integer = transactions.Length
```

We just called our index by the simple name "**i**" and set its value to the length of the transactions array. This will give us the index for the next item that we want to add to the end of the array. At the beginning of our program, the array length will be 0. This is also the index of the first element that we will add!

Now that we know what element is next in the array, we can use the **ReDim Preserve** method to add a transaction to our array:

```
ReDim Preserve transactions(i)
```

At this point, our **transactions** array has a single element located at index 0. Finally, we can add our transaction information to our new array element. We set the transaction's amount to the **dollarAmount** that was passed into our function, and the **time** to the current time (using the **Date.Now** method).

```
transactions(i).amount = dollarAmount
transactions(i).time = Date.Now
```

Now that we've created this helper function, let's turn our attention to the buttons!

Double-click on both the "Deposit" and "Withdrawal" in your form to create the button click event handlers for each button. Each time the user clicks on one of the buttons we want to add a new transaction using the **Value** of the **dollarAmount** control. For deposits this value should be positive (so it will add) and for withdrawals it should be negative (so it will subtract).

Here's the line of code to add to the **DepositButton** handler:

```
addTransaction(dollarAmount.Value)
```

Now you can do the same for the **WithdrawalButton**, this time using a negative dollar amount:

```
addTransaction(-dollarAmount.Value)
```

At this point, when you run your program, you will be able to deposit and withdraw from your piggy bank, but you will not be able to see your balance as it changes. You will add this functionality in the activity at the end of this chapter.

For now, if you want to see your transactions, place a breakpoint on the first line in the **addTransaction()** function. Then you can press one of the two buttons, step through the code and watch as another transaction is added to the array!

Here is the complete code for the three functions you just wrote:

```
Private Sub addTransaction(ByVal dollarAmount As Decimal)
  Dim i As Integer = transactions.Length
  ReDim Preserve transactions(i)
  transactions(i).amount = dollarAmount
  transactions(i).time = Date.Now
End Sub


Private Sub ButtonDeposit_Click(ByVal sender As System.Object, _
            ByVal e As System.EventArgs) Handles ButtonDeposit.Click


        addTransaction(dollarAmount.Value)
End Sub


Private Sub ButtonWithdrawal_Click(ByVal sender As System.Object, _
            ByVal e As System.EventArgs) Handles ButtonWithdrawal.Click
    addTransaction(-dollarAmount.Value)
End Sub
```

Right now when you run the program, you can click the two buttons to add or subtract money from the bank. But, other than watching things in the debugger, you can't really tell how your bank balance is changing. You will take care of that next in the chapter activity!

Chapter Review

- An array is a group of variables with the same data type and name.

- You can get or set each element in an array with a numeric index.

- Arrays indexes are zero-based, which means the first element in an array is element 0, not element 1.

- The length of an array is found by reading the array's **Length** property.

- Two-dimensional arrays hold a data grid.

- Two-dimensional arrays have two indexes: a column and a row.

- To change the size of an array in a program, you can use the **ReDim** keyword.

- To change the size of an array and keep the old information, use the **ReDim Preserve** keywords.

- A data structure is a way to create your own data type.

- A data structure can group variables and arrays together into one unit.

- You cannot set the size of an array in a data structure definition. You must use the **ReDim** statement after declaring your structure variable instead.

Your Turn: Viewing the Piggy Bank Statement

In this activity, you are going to change your Piggy Bank program so you can see all of the transactions and clear the transaction array.

Open the "PiggyBank" project you created in the last lesson. To do this, open up the Visual Basic IDE and click on "File" and "Open Project". Your project should have been saved in "C:\KidCoder\Windows Programming\My Projects\PiggyBank" and the filename should be "PiggyBank.sln". Select this file to open the project. If you do not see your project's screen and code, just use the icons on the Solution Explorer to show the screens.

First, add two new buttons to your form:

- A button with the **(Name)** "ViewButton" and the **Text**: "View Statement"
- A button with the **(Name)** "EmptyButton" and the **Text**: "Empty Bank"

Your form should look something like this:

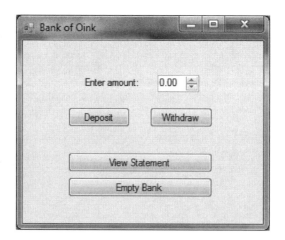

Now you will need to add some code to your new buttons. The "View Statement" button will show a message with all of the transactions in the array. You will display both the time and the amount of each transaction to the user with a **MsgBox**.

Add the following code to the **ViewButton** click event handler function:

- Create a **String** variable called **statement** to hold the statement output
- Create a **Decimal** variable called **balance** to hold the total balance for the bank and set the initial value to 0.0
- Create a **For** loop to loop over the entire transaction array
- Inside the loop, do the following:
  - Add the transaction's **time** to the **statement** string
  - Add a space and a dollar sign to the **statement** string, then add the transaction's **amount**
  - Also add the **amount** to the balance variable to keep a running total
  - Make the statement "wrap" to the next line by adding the **vbNewLine** special character.
- When the **For** loop has completed, add one last line to your **statement** variable – the final balance! Add the text "Current Balance: $" and then the **balance** amount to your **statement**.
- Finally, use a **MsgBox** to show the contents of the **statement** variable

Now run your program and try out this button! Here is an example statement with three transactions – a deposit of $1.00, then a deposit of $5.00, and then a withdrawal of $3.00. The current balance after all transactions is $3.00.

There is only one button left, and that is the "Empty Bank" button. As you might guess, you want this button to remove all entries from your transactions array. Find or create the click handler function for this button. Then add some code to remove all of the elements from the **transactions** array. Here's a hint: you can do this with one line of code and the **ReDim** keyword!

When finished, run your program and try out the "Empty Bank" button. First add some transactions and view the statement. Then click the "Empty Bank" button and view the statement again. When you click on the "View Statement" button after emptying the bank, you should see a one-line statement with a balance of $0.

Chapter Thirteen: Distributing Your Programs

In this chapter we will show how one of your programs can be installed on other computers.

Lesson One: What Your Program Needs To Run

Once you have created your program masterpiece, there is only one thing left to do: share it with the world! In this lesson, we will discuss the files that are needed to make your program run on another computer.

Executable File

An executable program file is created for you every time you build your project. This file has an ".EXE" on the end of it and can be found in your project directory under the "bin\Debug" or "bin\Release" sub-folder.

For example, take a look at the "Pig Latin Translator" project you created in an earlier chapter. Run the Windows Explorer and go to your "Pig Latin Translator\bin\Debug" directory:

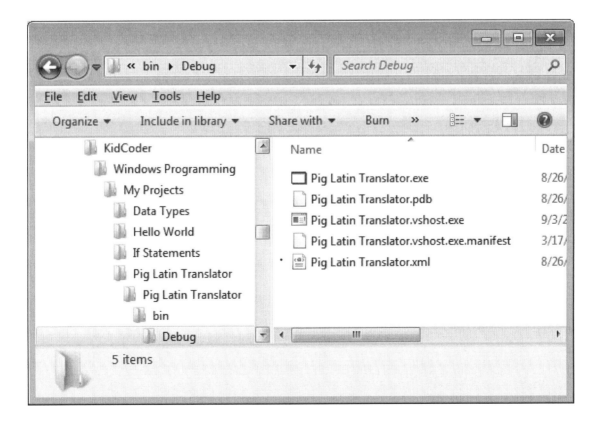

In the "KidCoder\Windows Programming\MyProjects\Pig Latin Translator\Pig Latin Translator \bin\Debug" directory, you would find a file called "Pig Latin Translator.exe". To run this program from Windows Explorer you can just double-click on it, and the "Pig Latin Translator" will start!

But what if you wanted to share this program with your best friend? Can you just copy the "Pig Latin Translator.exe" file to their computer? The answer is no! A Visual Basic program (and almost all other types of programs) will require extra files or libraries to be installed on a computer before a program will run. These files are commonly called *dependencies*, since a program is dependent on (or needs) them to run correctly.

.NET Framework Dependency

At the very least, every Visual Basic program requires the .NET Framework library to be installed on a computer before the program will run. All of our programs will require this library in order to run properly. The .NET Framework was installed for you (if not already present) when you installed Visual Basic 2010 Express. However your friends may need to install the .NET Framework separately on their computers. This is a free download from Microsoft, and many computers already have it installed.

Other Dependency Files

Your program may also need other files that are special to that program. For example, you might have graphics files, or sound files, or even databases that are used by your program. If your program needs other files, these will need to be copied to the other computer along with your program before your program will run.

Once you have copied over your executable file, and made sure the .NET Framework is installed, and copied over any other dependencies, you are ready to run your program on another computer!

Lesson Two: Distributing to the Public

If you can't just copy the executable file to another computer, how do you get your program running on your friend's computer? To do this, we will use a method called "Publishing". This method will create a "setup.exe" file which will allow you to install your program on any other computer.

The first step in publishing your program is to add some settings in your project properties. These settings will determine how the program looks on the "Start" menu after it is installed.

To access these properties, open the Visual Basic project and then click on "Project" and "Properties" on the menu at the top of the screen:

This will open the properties window for the current project. In our case, this is the "Pig Latin" program.

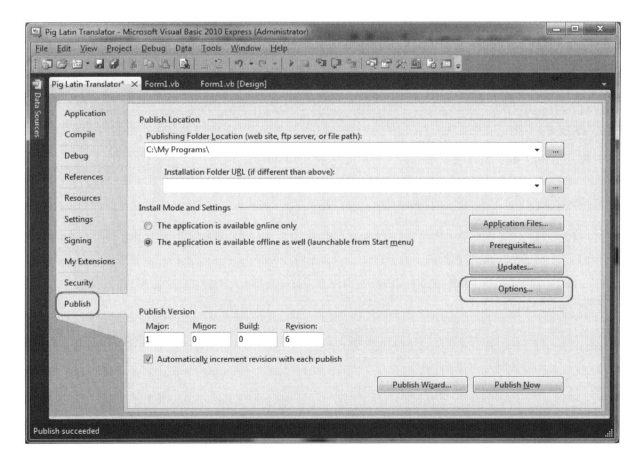

You will need to click on the tab on the left side of the screen that is labeled: "Publish". Then click on the "Options" button that will appear on the right side of the screen.

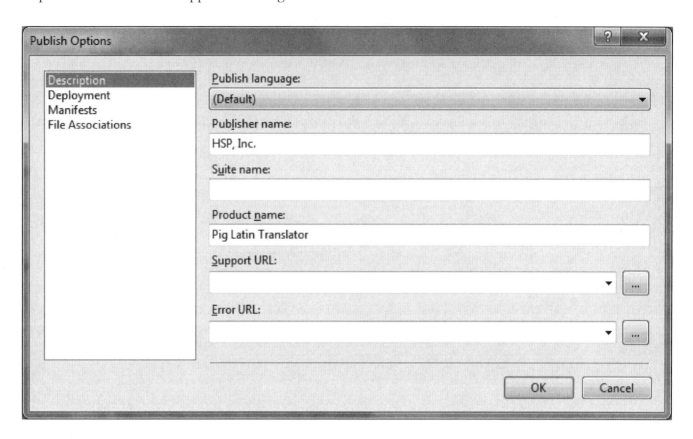

The options dialog has a number of fields, and two of these are important for our program: the "Publisher name" and the "Product Name". The "Publisher name" is the name of the folder that will contain your program in the Start menu. In our case, we named this "HSP, Inc.". You can name this "Joe's Software", "NateWare", or any other name that you would like to use for your software.

The "Product name" is the name of the program that will appear in the "HSP, Inc" (or other Publisher name) folder. Here, we named our program the "Pig Latin Translator".

Make sure you click on the "OK" button to save your changes!

Publishing the Program

To publish your program, click on the "Project" Menu and then "Publish <Program Name>". You will see a screen like the one below:

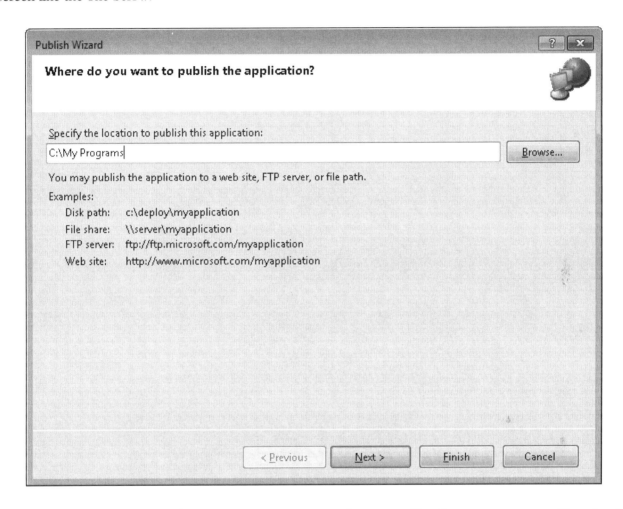

From here, you can choose where you want to output the setup files for your program. The simplest method is to choose a directory on your computer's hard drive (such as "C:\My Programs"), but you can also choose to send the setup files straight to a website or an FTP server.

For now, let's stick with a directory on your computer's hard drive.

When you click on the "Next" button, you will see the following screen:

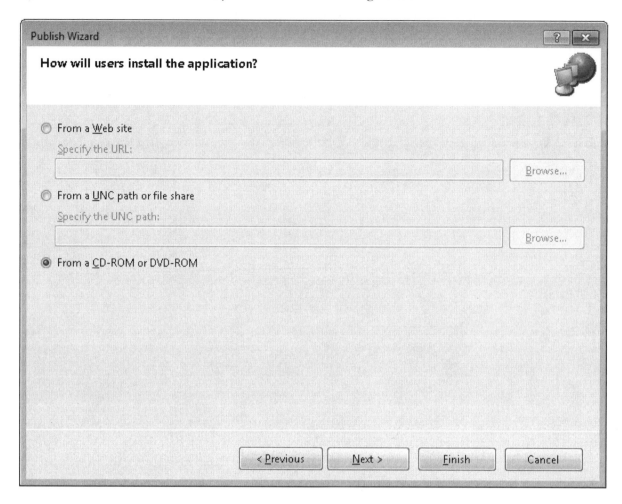

On this screen, you need to decide how other people will get your setup files. You should usually just pick the "From a CD-ROM or DVD-ROM" option. This option is the most popular since it will allow you to save the files to a CD or DVD and then hand out the disc directly to your other users.

This method will not actually burn the setup files onto a disc, but it will just create the files which can then be copied or burned to a disc later.

The next screen will allow you to set a place where the program can check for updates. This is a great feature if you want your users to be able to download any fixes or patches for the program after it is installed. We will not be using this option in our programs, so select "The application will not check for updates".

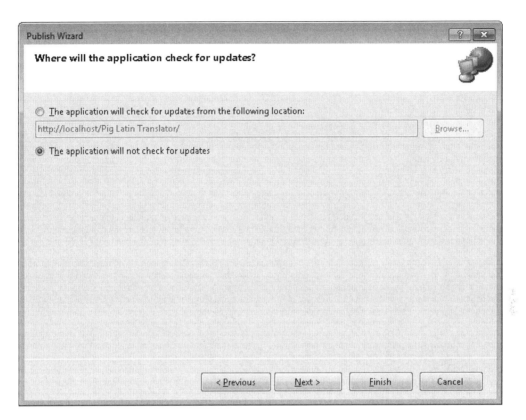

Click Next to get to the last screen!

The final screen is shown below. This screen allows you to double-check all of your settings before the setup files are created.

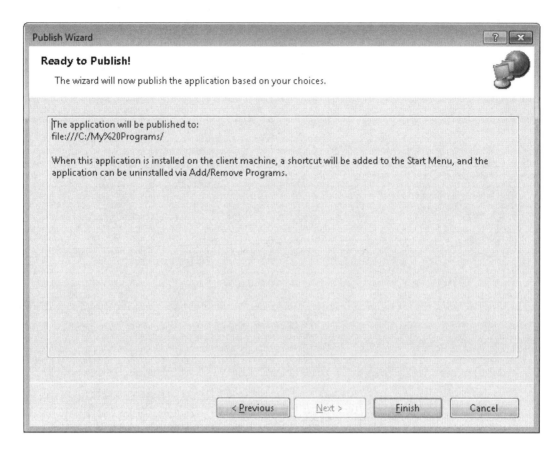

Once you click on the "Finish" button on the above screen, the project will be built and the setup files will be created. At the end of this process, you will end up with files like the ones shown below in the target "C:\My Programs" directory.

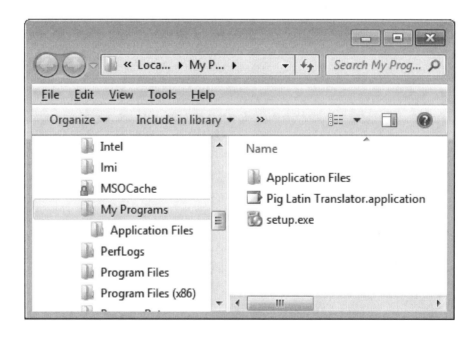

You can see under your target "My Programs" directory there is a "setup.exe" file, a "Pig Latin Translator.application" file, and an "Application Files" subdirectory. All of these items should then be copied to a CD, DVD, flash drive, or ZIP file so they can be moved to your target computer. You may also be able to copy the files directly across your home network.

When you get all of these files and folders copied to another computer, simply run the "setup.exe" program. It will install all the necessary files (including the .NET Framework library) and add a shortcut to the Start Menu. The program can then be run right from the Start menu.

You should note that this method does not create an "Un-Install" program. Your users will have to go to the Windows Control Panel screen and choose "Add/Remove Programs" or "Programs and Features" (depending on Windows version) to remove the program once it is installed.

Other Methods of Distribution

The methods of distributing a program mentioned above are the simplest and easiest for you to use. However, you may find that these methods don't offer some advanced features you need to install (or uninstall) your program. If this is the case, you may need to try a different setup tool. There are many tools on the market today, including professional tools that cost money, or freeware tools that are good for student or hobby programmers. These tools offer more than the options built into the Visual Basic IDE but are more difficult to use. We recommend using the publishing features that come with Visual Basic 2010 Express unless you have a strong reason to use some other tool.

Lesson Three: Installing and Un-Installing a Published Program

Now that you have your setup files, exactly how do you install the program on another computer? How would you then un-install them later?

Program Installation

The first installation step is to copy the files onto the target computer. This can be done with either a CD or DVD disc, or flash drive, ZIP file, by direct network copy, or some other way. The next step is to run the "setup.exe" file. Once this file is run, you should see a screen, similar to the following, appear for a few seconds:

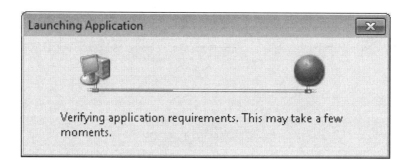

Once this screen is complete, it will disappear and you will see the following screen:

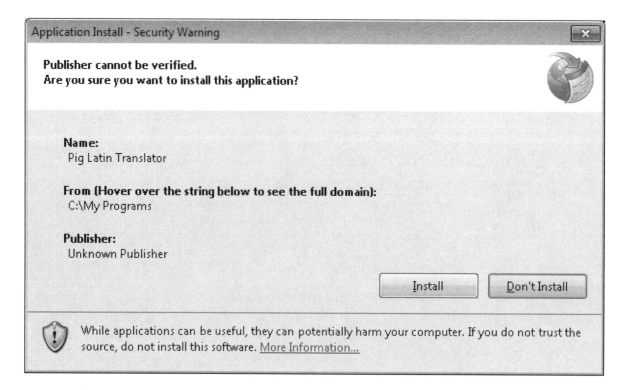

You will notice that there is a warning on the screen above. This warning is just telling the user that the program they are about to install does not come from a recognized Microsoft software publisher. Since you are just a student and not a large corporation, this is to be expected! When you see a message like this one, you should make sure that you trust the person that gave you the program and that you understand the program that you are installing. Then it is usually okay to continue with the installation.

When you click on the Install button, you will see the following screen:

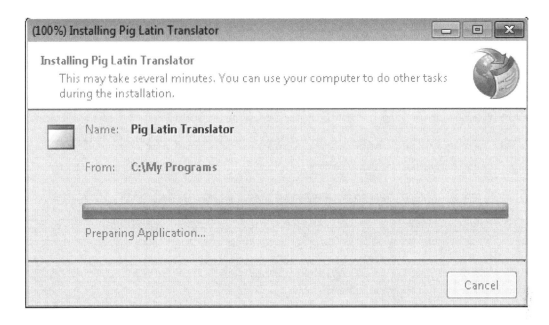

If your program is small (like our Pig Latin program), this window may appear and disappear so quickly that you miss it! Larger programs will require more time for installation.

Once the program is installed, it will automatically run and be seen on the computer:

The Start Menu

After your program is installed, you should be able to find it on your Windows Start menu. Depending on your version of Windows, your "Start" button could look like the samples below:

Once you click on this button, a list of programs and program folders should appear. Your program will be listed under the folder with the same name as the "Publisher Name" we set in the Publish properties. Inside this folder will be your program:

If you click on the program name, the program should start and appear on your screen.

In addition, you may find your program "pinned" to the start menu, like this:

Un-Installing the Program

As we mentioned in an earlier lesson, there is no "un-install" program created when you publish a program. Instead, a user will need to open up the Windows Control Panel and choose the "Add or Remove Programs" icon. At that point, the operating system will display a list of programs that are currently installed on the computer. The list of programs and the look-and-feel of the list of programs will vary from computer to computer and between Windows versions. The screen below shows one example:

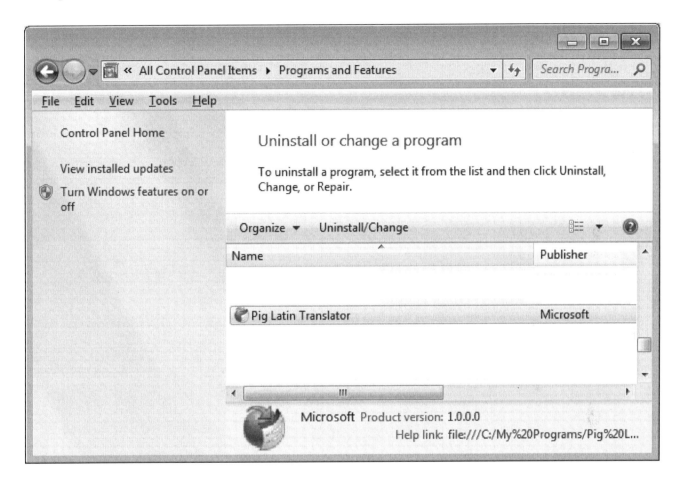

You can see that the "Pig Latin Translator" application is highlighted. In the bar above the list of programs, there is a button called "Uninstall/Change". Depending on your version of Windows, you may see a button called "Change/Remove" instead. Either of these buttons will allow you to remove this program from this computer. If you click on the button, you will see the following screen:

Once you click on the "OK" button, the "Pig Latin Translator" program will be uninstalled from this computer. It's as easy as that!

 **Chapter Review**

- A Visual Basic program cannot be distributed to another user's computer by copying only the executable file.

- Visual Basic programs need other files called dependencies.

- The programs that we are writing in this course require the .NET Framework library to be installed on any computer that runs our programs.

- The Visual Basic 2010 Express software contains a simple "publish" method to create a setup file for our programs.

- When you choose to "publish" your program, the IDE creates a "setup.exe" and other files and directories that are needed to install all dependencies on another computer.

- The "publish" method does not create an "un-install" program. If a user wants to un-install the program, they will need to do this through the "Add or Remove Programs" button in the Control Panel.

Your Turn: Publish a Program

In this activity, you will publish one of the programs that you have created in this course. You may choose any of the earlier chapter programs that you would like to publish.

Open the chapter program you picked in the Visual Basic 2010 Express software.

In order to publish the program, you will have to do the following:

- Change the Publish Options to show the correct "Publisher name" and "Product name" for your program.
- Click on the "Build" menu and then "Publish <Program Name>" option. (Where <Program Name> is the name of the program that you are publishing.)
- Choose a directory to publish the files. We suggest "C:\KidCoder\Windows Programming\My Installs", but you can choose any location on your hard drive.
- Create an install for a CD or DVD as described in this chapter.
- After the publishing is complete, check your target directory to make sure the setup files have been created.
- Test the install on your own computer or on another computer!

After you are done with this activity you can use the Windows Control Panel to un-install your program as described in the last lesson.

Chapter Fourteen: Putting It All Together

In this final chapter we will combine all that you have learned to write a simple game!

The following screen from a game called Pong™ may look familiar to you:

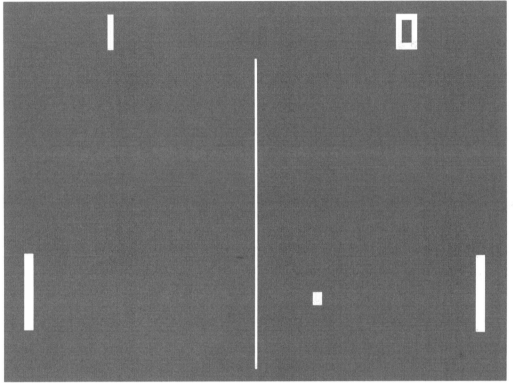

The original Pong™ game

Pong™ was a very popular video game back in the early 1970s. This game was something like ping-pong with two players hitting a ball back and forth across the screen. The ball would bounce at different angles off the "walls" of the screen and off the opponent's "paddle". A simple scoreboard would record how many times each player had hit the ball. The graphics were very simple. The "paddles" were two long, thin rectangles and the "ball" was a small square dot.

In this chapter you will use your Visual Basic skills to create a simple, one-player version of Pong™!

Lesson One: Understanding Screen Coordinates

Every computer screen is broken down into a grid of tiny blocks called pixels. To explain how the computer uses this grid, let's take a look at a common type of grid, a tic-tac-toe board.

X		O
	O	
X		X

A tic-tac-toe board is a grid that has 3 blocks across and 3 blocks down, for a total of 9 blocks. When people are playing this game, they just simply look at the board and draw their X or O in one of the blocks. If you are playing tic-tac-toe with a computer, however, it gets a little more complicated. A computer cannot "see" the board, so how does it know where to draw its X or O?

The computer would use numbers to represent spaces in the tic-tac-toe board. There are two numbers for each square: a column value, which tells the computer how far over from the left to draw its letter, and a row value, which tells the computer how far down from the top to draw its letter.

Let's look at the column (or horizontal) value in our tic-tac-toe grid. This value is called the "X" coordinate:

0	1	2

The x-coordinate values will always start at 0 and increase as you move right in the grid. This value literally tells the computer how many spaces a block is from the left.

Now let's look at the row (or vertical) value in our tic-tac-toe board. This value is called the "Y" coordinate:

0
1
2

The y-coordinate values will also always start at 0 and increase as you move down the board. This value tells the computer how far down a block is from the top.

When these two values are put together in a pair, they work as an address for the block that the computer can easily understand.

Let's look at our tic-tac-toe board again with the addresses (X-Y coordinate pairs) in each square:

0,0	1,0	2,0
0,1	1,1	2,1
0,2	1,2	2,2

A computer screen is much like a tic-tac-toe board, only bigger! The "blocks" on your computer screen are called "pixels" and there are usually at least 800 columns and 600 rows. Just like the blocks in the tic-tac-toe board, each pixel has an X and Y coordinate that the computer uses to place objects on the screen. When we create our "Pong™" game, we will be using these values to tell the computer where to draw our ball and paddle. By making small changes to these coordinates we can make the objects move across the screen.

Lesson Two: Starting Your Game

The first thing you will need to do is create a new project in the Visual Basic IDE called "MyPong". Once this project is created, change the Form **(Name)** to "PongForm" and the **Text** to "My Pong Game". You will probably want to make the form a little bigger than the default size. This is the playing field for your game, so you will want to have some room to play!

We will need a few simple controls on our form: a "Start" button, a label for the user's score, and two shapes. We'll get to the shapes in a second; for now just add a button and a label to your form. Change the button's **(Name)** to "StartButton" and the **Text** to "Start". Change the label's **Name** to "ScoreLabel" and its **Text** to "Current Score: 0". Move the **StartButton** to the bottom of the form and the label to the top right of the form.

We will also be adding two shape controls to our form. The shape control can be found in the Control Toolbox under the section called "Visual Basic Power Packs". You will need to create one "OvalShape" control and one "RectangleShape" control. Change the "OvalShape" control's **(Name)** to "PongBall" and the "RectangleShape" control's **(Name)** to "PongPaddle".

 **Your Visual Basic 2010 Express should already have the "Power Packs" section in your toolbox. Rarely, the Power Packs can be missing for some reason. If you cannot find them, please check the support area of our website for instructions on getting the Power Packs installed!**

You will need to adjust the size of these shapes until your oval is more of a circle and about a quarter-inch wide, and your rectangle is about an inch wide and a quarter-inch high. In order to see the ball better, let's change its color. Look for the **FillColor** property for the **PongBall**. Click in the property area and you will see a pop-up box that has tabs on top of it. Choose the "Custom" tab and then pick a color. (We chose red, but you can pick any color.) To make this color fill the circle, look for the **FillStyle** property and select "Solid" from the list. Then do the same thing for the **PongPaddle** control. Choose the **FillColor** property and set it to a color (we chose black) and then set its **FillStyle** to "Solid".

For the Pong game to work, you will need to move your "PongPaddle" down to the bottom of the screen.

Your form should now look something like the one shown on the right.

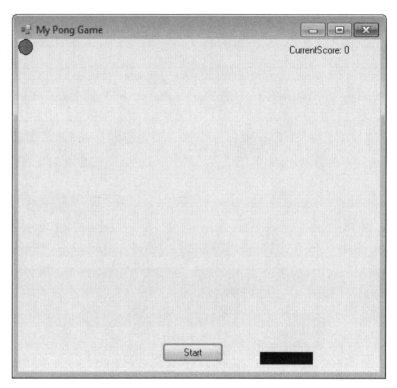

Now let's add some code to our Pong program! Open up the code window for your form. Just below the line "Public Class PongForm" you will add a couple of variables for our program to use.

Create two **Integer** variables: "**xDirection**" and "**yDirection**". We will use these variables to make our "PongBall" move around the screen. Next create a third **Integer** variable called "**currentScore**". This variable will be used to keep track of our user's score.

Your code so far should look like this:

```
Public Class PongForm
        'These variables hold the ball's current direction and speed
        Dim xDirection, yDirection As Integer

        'This variable holds the currentScore for the user
        Dim currentScore As Integer
End Class
```

Now we will add some code to make our **PongPaddle** rectangle move back and forth on the screen when the user moves the mouse. To do this, look at the top of your code window. You should see two drop-down boxes at the top. Click on the arrow to the right of the first box and choose the "(PongForm Events)" item. Then click on the arrow on the right of the second box and choose "MouseMove".

This should create a new **Sub** called **PongForm_MouseMove**(). This subroutine will be called every time a user moves their mouse. We will use it to make our **PongPaddle** move too!

Here is what your new **Sub** looks like:

```
Private Sub PongForm_MouseMove(ByVal sender As Object, _
               ByVal e As System.Windows.Forms.MouseEventArgs) _
               Handles Me.MouseMove


End Sub
```

The second parameter of **PongForm_MouseMove**() is "**e**", declared as type **System.Windows.Forms. MouseEventArgs**. This variable contains information about the user's mouse position. The properties ".**X**" and ".**Y**" contain the mouse's current screen coordinates. What we want to do is make the pong paddle move left and right wherever the mouse cursor goes. We can update the pong paddle's position by getting the "**e.X**" coordinate of the mouse and doing some math. This math will set the paddle's position so the middle of the paddle is in line with the mouse cursor!

Enter the following code within the **PongForm_MouseMove**() Sub:

```
'When the user moves their mouse, we will move our paddle to match
PongPaddle.Left = e.X - PongPaddle.Width / 2
```

Let's look at the first part of this statement: "**PongPaddle.Left**". The **PongPaddle**.Left property controls where the left side of the rectangle starts on the screen. When we set it equal to some value, we are moving the whole **PongPaddle** rectangular control so that the left edge starts at the **Left** property value.

We could simply set "**PongPaddle.Left = e.X**", which would move the paddle so that the left edge was in line with the mouse cursor. But it would feel more natural to the user if the paddle moved so that the middle of the paddle was in line with the mouse cursor. To do this, we can simply subtract half the paddle width (**PongPaddle.Width / 2**) from the mouse position **e.X** and assign that result to the **.Left** paddle property.

Now try it out! Run your program and watch as the "paddle" follows your mouse movements from left to right.

 **Make sure you remember to save your project when you close the application. To do this, click on "File" and "Close Project". Name your project "My Pong", make sure you are saving in your "C:\KidCoder\Windows Programming\My Projects" directory, and name your solution "My Pong".**

You will be adding to this project over several lessons, so make sure to save your code each time you reach a stopping point!

Lesson Three: Using the Timer Control to Animate the Screen

In this lesson, we will make our **PongBall** circle move around the screen. To make the ball move smoothly, we actually want to make many small changes to the position every second! In order to do this, we would like to have some function that automatically gets called very quickly, so we can change the position each time the function is called. Fortunately, Visual Basic has a "Timer" control that will do exactly what we need!

A "Timer" control makes a subroutine call at regular times, and within that subroutine you can write your game logic! We will use the timer to move our "PongBall" about 30 times every second (which is once every 33 milliseconds).

Make sure the "MyPong" project is open and the "PongForm" is displayed on the screen. Then find the "Timer" in the Control Toolbox under the "Components" section and double-click it to add it to your form. You will notice that it does not show up on your form, but is in a little gray rectangle with a clock labeled "Timer1" at the bottom of the form window! This is because a "Timer" control is not visible on the screen; it just runs in the background of your program.

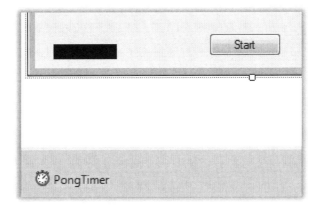

Look at the property sheet for the "Timer" control and change the **(Name)** to "PongTimer". You can also see the **Interval** property for this control. For our program, set this interval to "33" to make the function call every 33 milliseconds.

Now let's add some code to our new control by double-clicking on the "PongTimer". This should open the code window and create a new **Sub** called **PongTimer_Tick**(). (If it didn't, just open the code window and choose "PongTimer" in the left drop-down box, and "Tick" in the right drop-down box.) This **Sub** will be called 30 times every second, giving us a chance to move the ball around the screen.

Here is a list of the things we want to do every time the **Tick**() sub is run:

- Move the ball using the current direction and speed, bouncing off the top or side if needed

- If the bottom of the ball has reached the top of the paddle:
    - If the ball has missed the paddle:
        - Stop the timer and pause the game
    - Else: They have hit the ball with the paddle!
        - Increase the user's current score by 1 point
        - Set a new direction for the ball based on where it hits the paddle
        - Make the ball go faster each time they hit it

The outline above shows you what the main **If** statement should look like in this function.

The first task is to move the ball a small amount in its current direction. If the ball hits the top or one of the sides we need to bounce it in another direction.

The next task is to see if the ball has fallen down to the same level as the paddle. If it has, check to see if the paddle has missed the ball. If they missed, then the game is over.

If the paddle hits the ball, we want to increase the user's score by 1 point and bounce the ball back up in a different direction. To add some challenge to the game we will make the new ball direction depend on where they hit it with the paddle. We will also make the ball go faster each time they hit it.

We could code all of this logic directly within the **PongTimer_Tick**() subroutine. However that would result in a very large, hard-to-read block of code! We will create subroutines to perform each of the tasks. Calling these subroutines from the **PongTimer_Tick**() subroutine will make that code smaller and easier to follow.

We will write most of the **If** logic in the next lesson. For now, we will work on the first line: moving the ball!

Moving the Ball

First let's create a new subroutine to move the ball. Find the line "**End Class**" at the bottom of the code window and add our new **Sub** just above this line. Let's call our new **Sub** "**MoveBall**". Go ahead and create the **Sub** declaration like this:

```
Private Sub MoveBall ()
```

We will call the **MoveBall()** function from within the **PongTimer_Tick()** subroutine. That means **MoveBall()** will be called 30 times a second because that's how often our timer control will call **PongTimer_Tick()**. Each time **MoveBall()** is called we want to move the ball just a little bit. Moving an object on the screen by just a few pixels many times a second will give the illusion of smooth motion.

Remember that we created two variables at the top of the Form called **xDirection** and **yDirection**. These variables will hold the number of pixels to add or subtract from the ball's current X and Y coordinates. If **xDirection = 1** and **yDirection = 1**, that means the ball's X and Y coordinates will increase by one, moving the ball down and to the right. If the **xDirection** is negative then the ball will move to the left. If the **yDirection** is negative then the ball will move up. If **xDirection** and/or **yDirection** are greater than 1, then the ball will move faster (more spaces) on each timer tick.

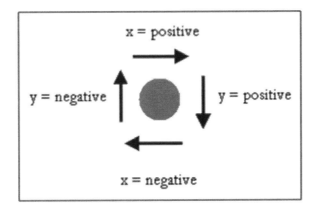

The first thing we want to do in our **MoveBall()** subroutine is check the current ball position and "bounce" it in another direction if it has hit the top or sides of the screen.

We can see if the ball has hit the top by checking if the **PongBall.Top** property is less than or equal to zero. Remember, a zero Y coordinate represents the first row of pixels across the top of the screen. Enter this code in your **MoveBall()** subroutine:

```
'Check to see if the ball has reached the top of the screen
If (PongBall.Top <= 0) Then
    yDirection = yDirection * -1
End If
```

If the ball has reached the top, we use a neat trick to bounce the ball off the top of the screen. For the ball to have reached the top, it must have been moving up, so the **yDirection** must be negative. We will just multiply the **yDirection** by -1 to change it to a positive value. We want to change the direction (sign of the integer) without altering the speed (value of the integer). So, for example, if **yDirection** was -6 (moving upwards) and you multiply it by -1, the result is +6, which means the ball will then move downwards with the same speed.

Next, we want to check and see if the left edge of the ball has reached the left side of the screen. If it has, we can bounce it back to the right by multiplying the **xDirection** by -1 to reverse its direction (just like bouncing off the top!). Enter this code in **MoveBall**() next:

```
    'Check to see if the ball has reached the left of the screen
If (PongBall.Left <= 0) Then
        xDirection = xDirection * -1
End If
```

Finally, we check to see if the ball has reached the right of the screen. If it has, we also multiply the "**xDirection**" by -1 to reverse its direction and bounce it back to the left.

```
    'Check to see if the ball has reached the right of the screen
If (PongBall.Left + PongBall.Width >= Me.Width) Then
        xDirection = xDirection * -1
End If
```

There are a couple of special things in the above **If**() statement that should be explained. First, there is no **Right** property for the Pong Ball. We have the **Left** and **Width**, so we need to calculate the coordinate of the right edge by adding them together. Second, we need to know how wide the screen is, in pixels. Fortunately that value can be found by reading the **Width** property of "**Me**" ("**Me**" is an object which represents the current form window). So the above **If**() statement will evaluate to **True** if the right edge of the ball is greater than or equal to the right edge of the screen.

At this point we have checked the ball position against the top and both sides. The direction of the ball, as controlled by the **xDirection** and **yDirection** variables, has been changed if necessary to bounce the ball away from whatever side it hit.

Now to move the ball we simply add the current **xDirection** to the PongBall's **Left** property and the **yDirection** to the PongBall's **Top** property:

```
PongBall.Left = PongBall.Left + xDirection
PongBall.Top = PongBall.Top + yDirection
```

That's the end of our **MoveBall**() function! Let's call this new subroutine from **PongTimer_Tick**(). Go up to the **PongTimer_Tick**() sub and add the following line as the first statement:

```
MoveBall()
```

Starting the Game

Now that we have completed our **MoveBall**() code, let's add some code to the **StartButton** that will turn on our **PongTimer** and start the game. Create the event handler sub for the **StartButton** by double-clicking on the button on the form.

```
        Private Sub StartButton_Click(ByVal sender As System.Object, _
                        ByVal e As System.EventArgs) _
                        Handles StartButton.Click


        End Sub
```

When the user clicks the "Start" button on the screen, we need to initialize the position and direction of our ball and start the timer.

First set the initial position of the ball by setting the PongBall's **Top** and **Left** properties:

```
    PongBall.Top = 1
    PongBall.Left = 1
```

Next we want to set the ball's initial direction and speed. If **xDirection** and **yDirection** are both positive, the ball will begin moving down and to the right. We will choose a value of 2 for both directions in order for the ball to move slowly (but not too slowly!) at first:

```
    xDirection = 2
    yDirection = 2
```

Finally, we need to turn on our **PongTimer**. We use the **Enabled** property to turn a Timer on or off. If the **Enabled** property is **True**, the Timer is on, if it is **False**, the Timer is off. So, add this code to turn the Timer on:

```
    PongTimer.Enabled = True
```

Now let's test it out and see what happens! Go ahead and run the program.

After you click the Start button, you see the ball "fall" down the screen. Cool, right? But it will only do this once. In our next lesson, we will add the code that will allow the ball to bounce off the paddle!

Lesson Four: Hitting or Missing the Ball

In this lesson, we will add some code to make the "PongBall" bounce off the "PongPaddle". Open up the code window and look at the **PongTimer_Tick**() function again. After the call to **MoveBall**(), we want to check and see if the bottom of the ball has reached the top of the paddle. If it has, then we will decide if the ball hit or missed the paddle.

Add this **If** statement after the call to **MoveBall**() to check and see if the bottom of the ball is has hit or gone past the top of the paddle:

```
'If the bottom of the ball has reached the top of the paddle
If (PongBall.Top + PongBall.Height >= PongPaddle.Top) Then
```

Since there is no **Bottom** property for **PongBall**, we have to calculate the position of the bottom of the ball ourselves. We just add the ball height (**PongBall.Height**) to the **Top** of the ball to give us the Y coordinate of the bottom of the ball. Then we check to see if that position is greater than or equal to the **Top** of the **PongPaddle**. If it is, then the ball has either hit the paddle or gone past it (missed it).

Finding Hits and Misses

If the ball has reached the paddle, we will then check to see if they missed the ball. Add the following code inside the **Then** block for the above **If** statement:

```
'If the ball has missed the paddle
If (PongBall.Left + PongBall.Width < PongPaddle.Left) Or _
    (PongBall.Left > PongPaddle.Left + PongPaddle.Width) Then
```

Note: You will need to either enter this statement all on one line, or add an underscore (_) after the **Or** keyword to tell Visual Basic that our statement continues on the next line. This is a long **If** statement, so let's look at it part-by-part!

The first condition is "(**PongBall.Left** + **PongBall.Width** < **PongPaddle.Left**)". Here we are checking to see if the right side of the ball (**PongBall.Left** + **PongBall.Width**) went to the left of the paddle (**PongPaddle.Left**). If the right side of the ball is less than the left side of the paddle, that means the entire ball is to the left of the paddle and was missed! The picture below shows this case with the left-most ball, which has missed the paddle. We drew some imaginary lines so you can see the coordinates you are calculating for the rightmost side of the ball and the leftmost side of the paddle.

The second condition is "(**PongBall**.Left > **PongPaddle**.Left + **PongPaddle**.Width)". Here we are checking to see if the left side of the ball (**PongBall.Left**) went to the right of the paddle (**PongPaddle.Left** + **PongPaddle.Width**). If the left side of the ball is greater than the right side of the paddle, that means the entire ball is to the right of the paddle and was missed! This case is shown by the rightmost ball in the picture above.

Since either of these two conditions will mean that the user has missed the ball, we combine the expressions with the **Or** keyword. If either expression is **True** we want to stop the game. There may be a few tasks associated with stopping the game, so let's create a new subroutine to handle those tasks. Just above our last **Sub MoveBall**(), create a **Sub** called **PauseGame**():

```
Private Sub PauseGame()
End Sub
```

For now, within this subroutine we will just stop the timer when the user misses the ball:

```
PongTimer.Enabled = False
```

We'll come back to this function later when putting some finishing touches on the game. For now, we just want to call this function from our **PongTimer_Tick**() function when the ball is missed. Within the **Then** block of our **If** statement where we checked to see if the user missed the paddle, add the following line:

```
PauseGame()
```

Your **PongTimer_Tick**() Sub should now look like this:

```
MoveBall()

    'If the bottom of the ball has reached the top of the paddle
    If (PongBall.Top + PongBall.Height >= PongPaddle.Top) Then

        'If the ball has missed the paddle
        If (PongBall.Left + PongBall.Width < PongPaddle.Left) Or _
            (PongBall.Left > PongPaddle.Left + PongPaddle.Width) Then

            ' Stop the timer and pause the game
            PauseGame()
        End If
    End If
```

Now, what happens if the user **did** hit the ball with the paddle? In **PongTimer_Tick**(), we will add an **Else** statement on the inner **If** that evaluated to **True** when the user missed. The **Else** statements will be executed when that **If** statement evaluates to **False**, meaning the user hit the ball. Before the **End If** of the inner **If** statement, add the **Else**:

```
            'If the bottom of the ball has reached the top of the paddle
            If (PongBall.Top + PongBall.Height >= PongPaddle.Top) Then

                'If the ball has missed the paddle
                If (PongBall.Left + PongBall.Width < PongPaddle.Left) Or _
                    (PongBall.Left > PongPaddle.Left + PongPaddle.Width) Then

                    ' Stop the timer and pause the game
                    PauseGame()

                Else 'they have hit the ball with the paddle!

                End If
            End If
```

When the paddle hits the ball there are a few things we want to do within the above **Else** statement block. First, we add one to their current score. Second, we need to bounce the ball back up toward the top of the screen. Third, we want to increase the ball speed.

Updating the User Score

When the user's score changes we need to update the **currentScore** variable and then reflect that new value in the **ScoreLabel** text on the screen. To do this, we will create a new function that will create a **String** with the new score. We will use a function since we will return the updated label text from the function. Move your cursor down the program to the line just before our **MoveBall**() function. We will add our new function here. Let's call this new function **AddToScore**(), give it one **Integer** parameter and a **String** return value.

```
        Private Function AddToScore (pointScored As Integer) As String

        End Function
```

Our new function will increase the value of **currentScore** by adding the number in the input variable **pointScored**. By making the amount of points scored a variable, you could later add some fancy logic to give the user bonus points for a long-running game. After calculating the current score, we create a text string with the new value and return it from the function. Add the following lines within your **AddToScore**() function:

```
Private Function AddToScore (pointScored As Integer) As String
    currentScore = currentScore + pointScored
    Return ("Current Score: " & currentScore)
End Function
```

Finally, we want to call this function each time the user hits the ball with the paddle. Go back up to our **PongTimer_Tick**()and use this function (just under our **Else** keyword) to update the score label:

```
'If the bottom of the ball has reached the top of the paddle
If (PongBall.Top + PongBall.Height >= PongPaddle.Top) Then

        'If the ball has missed the paddle
        If (PongBall.Left + PongBall.Width < PongPaddle.Left) Or _
        (PongBall.Left > PongPaddle.Left + PongPaddle.Width) Then

            ' Stop the timer and pause the game
            PauseGame()

        Else 'they have hit the ball with the paddle!
            ScoreLabel.Text = AddToScore(1)
        End If
End If
```

Bouncing the Ball off the Paddle

When the ball hits the paddle, we want to bounce the ball back upwards. We also want to change the horizontal movement (left or right) based on where they hit the ball on the paddle. If the ball hit on the right half of the paddle, the ball will go up and to the right. If the ball hit on the left half of the paddle, it will go up and to the left. As you can imagine this takes some math and logic, so we will create another subroutine called **BounceBall**() to avoid making the **PongTimer_Tick**() code too long. Move your cursor down the program to the line just before our **AddToScore**() function. Then add our **BounceBall**() sub here:

```
Private Sub BounceBall()
End Sub
```

In the **BounceBall**() subroutine we will see which side of the paddle the ball hit and decide which direction to send the ball. If the middle of the ball is to the left of the middle of the paddle, then we say the ball hit on the left side. Otherwise (else) the ball hit on the right side.

To see if the middle of the ball is on the left side of the paddle, enter this code inside **BounceBall**():

```
If (PongBall.Left + PongBall.Width / 2) < _
    (PongPaddle.Left + PongPaddle.Width / 2) Then
End If
```

The left side of this conditional statement ("**PongBall**.**Left** + **PongBall**.**Width** / 2") calculates the midpoint of the ball. We take the leftmost ball coordinate and add half of the width to find the midpoint. The next part of the expression ("**PongPaddle**.**Left** + **PongPaddle**.**Width** / 2") does exactly the same thing to find the midpoint of the paddle. Finally, we compare these two midpoints. If the middle of the ball is less than the middle of the paddle that means it hit on the left side...and the **If** statement evaluates to **True**.

If the ball has hit on the left side of the paddle, we want to make the ball go left. Remember that the **xDirection** variable controls the horizontal (left/right) direction and speed. If the ball is already going left, we don't have to do anything. If it was going right, we will multiply **xDirection** by -1 to reverse the direction without changing the speed.

Add this code within the **Then** block of the **If** statement we just created:

```
If xDirection > 0 Then      'if ball was going right
    xDirection = xDirection * -1     'make it go left
End If
```

So, if our **xDirection** was positive (greater than 0), the ball was going right, so we reverse the direction. If **xDirection** was negative the ball was already going left, so we don't need to do anything.

Now that we have the code for the ball hitting the left side of the paddle, we need to add some code for it hitting the right. Since our first **If**() statement checked to see if the ball hit on the left, we can use a matching **Else** keyword now that will run if the ball hit on the right instead.

```
Else    'the ball must be on the right of the paddle
```

If the ball has hit on the right side of the paddle, we want to make the ball go right (we want the **xDirection** to be positive). If the ball is already going right, we don't have to do anything. If it was going left, we will multiply **xDirection** by -1 to reverse the direction without changing the speed

```
    If xDirection < 0 Then      'if ball was going left
        xDirection = xDirection * -1     'make it go right
    End If
```

If the **xDirection** was negative (less than 0), the ball was going left, so we reverse the direction. If **xDirection** was positive the ball was going right, so we don't need to do anything.

Next, we want to make the ball move upwards because it has bounced off the paddle. After the last **End If** at the bottom of the subroutine, let's reverse the direction:

```
    ' reverse the y Direction so ball will go back up
    yDirection = yDirection * -1
```

This just changes the sign of the **yDirection** so it will now be negative instead of positive. Now the ball (which was going down) will move upward instead.

Here is how the completed code for the **BounceBall**() sub should look:

```
Private Sub BounceBall()

    'If the ball is hitting on the left side of the paddle
    If (PongBall.Left + PongBall.Width / 2) < _
        (PongPaddle.Left + PongPaddle.Width / 2) Then

        If xDirection > 0 Then 'if ball was going right
            xDirection = xDirection * -1 'make it go left
        End If

    Else 'the ball must be on the right of the paddle

        If xDirection < 0 Then  'if ball was going left
            xDirection = xDirection * -1 'make it go right
        End If
    End If

    ' reverse the y Direction so ball will go back up
    yDirection = yDirection * -1

End Sub
```

Finally, we want to call this function each time the user hits the ball with the paddle. Go back up to our **PongTimer_Tick**() sub and add a call to our **BounceBall**() sub after the call to **AddToScore**():

```
            'If the bottom of the ball has reached the top of the paddle
    If (PongBall.Top + PongBall.Height >= PongPaddle.Top) Then


        'If the ball has missed the paddle
        If (PongBall.Left + PongBall.Width < PongPaddle.Left) Or _
            (PongBall.Left > PongPaddle.Left + PongPaddle.Width) Then


            ' Stop the timer and pause the game
            PauseGame()

        Else 'they have hit the ball with the paddle!
            ScoreLabel.Text = AddToScore(1)
            BounceBall()
        End If
    End If
```

That's it! Now run the program, press the "Start" button, and try to hit the ball with the paddle! The ball should bounce correctly off the paddle, both sides, and the top of the form. If you miss the ball, the timer (and the ball) should stop.

Hint: We have added quite a few **If** statements to our code. Make sure that all of your **If** statements are properly ended with an **End If** statement. If your ball is not moving correctly, remember you can set a breakpoint in your **PongTimer_Tick** function, the **MoveBall** function, or the **BounceBall** function and then watch your program step-by-step in the debugger!

Lesson Five: Final Touches

In this lesson we will add some final touches to our "MyPong" project. We will add a function that speeds up the ball after every hit, and we will add some code that will hide the "Start" button when the game is playing and hide the ball and paddle when the game is paused.

Speeding up the Ball

Open up the code window for your game. We will add one more function to the program. This new function will use the **xDirection** and **yDirection** variables to speed up the ball when it is hit by the paddle. This adds a little difficulty to the game (and it was a key feature in the original Pong game).

Move your cursor down to the line just above the line "**End Class**". We will add our function above this line. Our subroutine will be called **SpeedUpBall()** and will look like this:

```
Private Sub SpeedUpBall()
```

The **xDirection** and **yDirection** variables are used to track the direction of the ball, but they can also be used to control the speed. If you increase the size (magnitude) of either of these variables, it will increase the speed. For example, a **yDirection** of +2 would move the ball slowly downwards, while a **yDirection** of +4 would move it downwards twice as fast!

We do not want to change the direction of the ball in this method, just increase the speed. Remember that either **xDirection** or **yDirection** could have a negative value (if the ball is traveling up or left) or a positive number (if the ball is traveling down or right). To increase a positive number, you add 1, to increase a negative number, you subtract 1. We will use two **If()** statements: one to change the **xDirection** and one to change the **yDirection**. Add this code inside **SpeedUpBall()** to handle the **yDirection** speed change:

```
If yDirection < 0 Then
        yDirection = yDirection - 1
Else
        yDirection = yDirection + 1
End If
```

First we check to see if the value of **yDirection** is negative (**yDirection < 0**). If it is negative, we increase the upward speed by subtracting 1. The **Else** statements will execute if **yDirection** is positive (moving downwards). If it is positive, we increase the downward speed by adding 1.

Our second **If** statement uses the same logic for the "**xDirection**" variable. Add this code inside **SpeedUpBall()** as well:

```
    If xDirection < 0 Then
        xDirection = xDirection - 1
    Else
        xDirection = xDirection + 1
    End If
```

Again, we check to see if the value of **xDirection** is negative (**xDirection** < 0). If it is negative, we increase the leftward speed by subtracting 1. If it is positive, we increase the rightward speed by adding 1.

That's it for this function! Now let's add a call to the function each time the user hits the ball. Go back up to our **PongTimer_Tick**() and add a call to **SpeedUpBall**()after the call to **BounceBall**():

```
    BounceBall()
    SpeedUpBall()
```

Now give it a try! This time the game should get harder the longer you play!

Hiding the Start Button

Finally, you may have noticed the annoying "Start" button hanging out on the screen during the game. We don't have to put up with that! Every button (and most controls in general) has a property called **Visible**. We will use this property to show or hide the "Start" button. While we're at it, we can change the **Visible** properties of our **PongBall** and **PongPaddle** to hide these controls when the game is paused and show them when the game is started.

Our existing subroutine **PauseGame**() is called each time the game stops. We will make this method show the **StartButton** and hide the **PongPaddle** and **PongBall** when the game is stopped. Under the line where the timer is stopped, add the following lines to make the **StartButton** visible, and the **PongPaddle** and **PongBall** invisible.

```
    'Show the Start button in case they want to play again
    StartButton.Visible = True

    'Hide the Paddle and the Ball
    PongPaddle.Visible = False
    PongBall.Visible = False
```

Next, when the game starts we want to make the pong paddle and ball visible and hide the start button. Look at the existing **StartButton_Click**() code. Here, after we set our initial position and speed for the ball and before we turn on the timer, add the following code:

```
'Make the paddle and the ball visible
PongPaddle.Visible = True
PongBall.Visible = True


'Hide the Start button
StartButton.Visible = False
```

This will make the paddle and ball visible and will hide the "Start" button when the game starts!

Setting the Initial Game State

Finally, we want to make sure that our program is in a "paused" state when the program starts. To do this, go back to the form design and double-click on the form itself (not on any controls). (Or, in the code window, you could choose "**PongForm Events**" in the left list box, and "**Load**" in the right list box.) This should bring up the code window with the **PongForm_Load**() function. This function will get called only one time: when the program first starts. This is a great place to call our **PauseGame**() function to set our initial values and hide everything except the "Start" button.

```
Private Sub PongForm_Load(ByVal sender As System.Object, _
                ByVal e As System.EventArgs) Handles MyBase.Load
    PauseGame()
End Sub
```

That's it! Run the program and play away! When the program first loads the ball and paddle should be hidden. When you click the "Start" button the button should hide and the ball and paddle will appear.

Your Turn: Double Your Trouble

The Pong game is cool, but we can make it much more exciting! In this activity, you will add a second ball to the game!

Open your "MyPong" project. To do this, run the Visual Basic IDE and click on "File" and "Open Project". Your project should have been saved in "C:\KidCoder\Windows Programming\My Projects\MyPong" and the filename should be "MyPong.sln". Select this file to open the project. If you do not see your project's screen and code, use the Solution Explorer icons to show the windows.

In order to add this second ball, you will have to do the following:

- Add a second "OvalShape" control that is the same size and shape as the first ball. (You can decide if you want the ball to be the same color or not). Name this new shape **PongBall2**. Make sure you use that new name whenever setting properties for the new ball.

- Add two new variables to handle the X and Y direction of the new ball.

- Copy the subroutines that control the first ball's movement on the screen into new subroutines that will move your second ball. Make sure the change the logic to use the new X and Y direction variables and **PongBall2**.

- Show the new ball and set its original position and speed in the **StartButton_Click**() function. Make sure the new ball's initial position is different than the old one! For instance, you could use "**Me.Width - PongBall2.Width**" as the starting **Left** property to put the new ball on the right side of the screen. You could also use "**Me.Height / 2**" as the starting **Top** property to position the ball half-way down the screen.

- Hide the new ball in the **PauseGame**() function

- Copy the **If**() statement in the **PongTimer_Tick**() function and modify the new copy to control the second ball.

You can also make other changes to your game if you like. Perhaps you could add to the bounce logic so it sends the ball off at different angles by changing the **xDirection** and **yDirection** differently. Or you could make the width of the paddle smaller after each bounce to make the game harder. Be creative!

What's Next?

Congratulations, you have finished *KidCoder*^{TM}*: Windows Programming*! This course was the first step in a series of exciting computer programming topics you can study. We encourage you to pursue the other courses available through Homeschool Programming, Inc.

The next course in the KidCoder^{TM} series is *KidCoder*^{TM}*: Game Programming*. In that course we will look at many different aspects of writing your own computer games in Visual Basic. The "My Pong" project in the final chapter of this course is merely an appetizer!

You may also choose to learn other programming languages such as C#. Other languages have their own strengths which you will discover over time. We offer a *TeenCoder*^{TM} series of courses geared for high school students. These courses teach you the C# language and also cover Windows and game programming topics in more depth.

We hope you have enjoyed this course produced by Homeschool Programming, Inc! We welcome student and teacher feedback at our website. Please also visit our website to request courses on other topics or see which new courses are available!

http://www.HomeschoolProgramming.com